LIVING BY STORIES

A Journey of Landscape and Memory

Harry Robinson

Compiled & Edited by Wendy Wickwire

Talonbooks
Vancouver

Talonbooks
P.O. Box 2076, Vancouver, British Columbia, Canada V6B 3S3
www.talonbooks.com

Typeset in Sabon and printed and bound in Canada.

First Printing: 2005

The publisher gratefully acknowledges the financial support of the Canada Council for the Arts; the Government of Canada through the Book Publishing Industry Development Program; and the Province of British Columbia through the British Columbia Arts Council for our publishing activities.

LIBRARY AND ARCHIVES CANADA CATALOGUING IN PUBLICATION

Robinson, Harry, 1900–1990.
  Living by stories : a journey of landscape and memory / Harry Robinson ; compiled and edited by Wendy Wickwire.

ISBN 0-88922-522-2

1. Okanagan Indians—Folklore. 2. Legends—British Columbia. 3. Indian mythology—British Columbia. I. Wickwire, Wendy C. II. Title.

E99.O35R6 2005   398.2'089'97943   C2005-902461-5

CONTENTS

EDITOR'S NOTE

I am grateful to Michael M'Gonigle, Alan Twigg, Karl Siegler, and Davinia Yip for their helpful comments on earlier drafts of the introduction. I would also like to thank Julie Cruikshank and Blanca Schorcht for their constant feedback and assistance on all things pertaining to Harry Robinson. My deep appreciation goes to my longtime friend and colleague, Lynne Jorgesen, Research Coordinator of the Upper Nicola Band Aboriginal Interest Project, Douglas Lake, BC. Although Lynne never met Harry, she devoured his stories while transcribing them for me fifteen years ago. She has many links to Harry's world, the most notable of which is her Okanagan Upper Nicola Band heritage. But another important one is her great grandmother, Nellie Guitterrez, who was one of the most beloved and respected elders in the southern Interior. A gifted writer and perfectionist with an insatiable passion for the history of her people, Lynne has always made time to attend to my nagging questions and concerns. There are no words that can adequately express my gratitude for the special assistance and support she gave me throughout the writing of the introduction.

Finally, this book is also dedicated to Karl and Christy Siegler for their continuing support.

INTRODUCTION

Harry Robinson lured me into Coyote's world. It happened on a baking hot day in mid-August 1977, during the initial leg of a week-long road trip through southern British Columbia. I was with three friends.[1] Our first stop was Harry's place just east of Hedley. As we pulled into his driveway, a series of stark contrasts came into view: in the distance, the mellow Similkameen River flowing through the dry valley dotted with sagebrush and ancient sun-scorched formations of volcanic rock; in the foreground, the frantic Highway 3, lined with heavy transport trucks and cars winging their way to points east and west. These contrasts became more apparent in Harry's front room where a large floor-to-ceiling picture window framed the details in glass.

Except for the hum of traffic, it was a tranquil scene. Harry's tiny, 1950s bungalow was one of only two houses for quite a distance. And, other than a few cats, his "boys," he was on his own. He was surprisingly agile, energetic, and independent for a man of seventy-seven. And he clearly enjoyed having visitors: he had prepared extra beds, anticipating that we would spend the night at his place.

When we had gathered around the Arborite table in his front room, one of us asked why there were no salmon in the local section of the Similkameen River. "That's a long long story," Harry explained. "It's all Coyote's fault." Suddenly it was as if Coyote was right there. Harry's easygoing demeanour changed. He stiffened, cleared his throat, and began telling us about Coyote's antics along the local rivers, peddling salmon in exchange for wives. All went well, Harry explained, until he encountered the Similkameen people who rejected his offers. Miffed, Coyote drove the salmon permanently out of the lower reaches of the river by creating an impassable barrier.

Except for the occasional cigarette break, Harry told this story without interruption or props beyond a continuous series of striking hand gestures that were choreographed to the narrative. As the blazing sky cooled into dusk while the earth continued to radiate the day's heat, the story consumed the evening. We sat transfixed, enjoying the travel back in time—who knows how far—to when the world was young and the landscape was first being formed and peopled. Harry broke from the storyline to point out tangible remains of Coyote's trip along the river, such as his pithouse near the present-day town of Princeton.

By the end of the evening, I was hooked on what felt like a direct encounter with Coyote—a *living* Coyote linked to Harry by generations of storytellers. Harry portrayed him as a bit of a pest. As he put it, "Coyote was a bad bad boy!" But I figured he could not have been all bad because Harry laughed endearingly while telling us of his "bad" doings. I wondered about common English terms for Coyote: trickster, transformer, vagabond, imitator, prankster, first creator, seducer, fool. A generation of established writers such as Paul Radin, Gary Snyder, Barry Lopez, and others had used these;[2] and yet Harry had not used a single one of them.

As we said our farewells late the next day, Harry invited us all to return. I assured him that I would. And I promised myself to first survey the ethnographies and oral narrative collections for this region to see how Harry's forebears had depicted Coyote. A number of anthropologists—James Teit, Leslie Spier, Charles Hill-Tout, Walter Cline, Rachel Commons, May Mandelbaum, Richard Post, and L. V. W. Walters—had travelled through the Okanagan region between 1888 and 1933 collecting stories.[3] So too had the Okanagan novelist Christine Quintasket (Mourning Dove) recorded traditional stories among her relatives and friends.[4] Franz Boas and Teit had also published several collections of stories of neighbouring Salishan-speaking peoples.[5]

I was pleased to discover numerous fragments of Harry's Coyote story scattered throughout the early collections. But the extensive variations among them made it impossible to find anything close to a single storyline. It was clear that Harry's predecessors had held conflicting views about Coyote's travels along the Similkameen. I skimmed the hundreds of Coyote stories featured in these collections: "Coyote Juggles His Eyes," "Coyote Fights Some Monsters," "Coyote, His Four Sons, and the Grizzly Bear," "Coyote Steals Fire," "Coyote and the Woodpeckers," "Coyote and the Flood," and so on. At the end of this survey, I did not feel particularly enlightened. In fact, Coyote seemed more contradictory and elusive than ever.

The print versions of these stories were short—on average, a page or two in length—and lifeless. Most lacked the detail, dialogue, and colour of Harry's story. Many were also missing some vital segments. Coyote's sexual exploits along the Similkameen River had been excised from the main text of an 1898 collection, translated into Latin and then transferred to endnotes.[6] Such editing seriously disrupted the integrity of the original narrative. Names of individual storytellers and their community affiliations were also missing, thus making it difficult to assess the roles of gender, geographical location, or individual artistry in shaping the stories. In many cases, collectors had created composite stories from multiple versions, which erased all sense of variation in the local storytelling traditions.

Despite these problems, merely surveying the published sources prepared me for my next session with Harry—or so I thought until I turned up at

Harry's house exactly two years later. I was with Nellie Guitterrez, a Douglas Lake elder who was also an old friend Harry had not seen in years. He was delighted to see us. I was relieved that he remembered me. At the end of this visit, I arranged to return the following week on my own.

During the latter visit, I brought up one of my favourite topics—James (Jimmy) Teit, a Shetlander based at Spences Bridge on the Thompson River. I wondered if Harry had met Teit before the latter's death in 1922. Teit had worked with New York-based anthropologist Franz Boas between 1894 and 1922. He had also served Aboriginal chiefs throughout the province in their campaign to resolve their land problems with European and American newcomers. I obviously struck a nerve because Harry began reconstructing the days of the "big meetings" (as he called them) attended by Teit at the behest of these chiefs. "Nowadays they call it the Land Question. Still going, you know." There was a problem with these "big meetings," he explained. Everyone had ignored how "Indians" had come "to be here in the first place":

The Indians, they don't say,
  they don't say *how come* for the Indians
    to be here first before the white.
See?
They never did tell that....
They never say *how come* for the Indians
  to belong to that what they have claimed...
How come the Indians to own this place
  and how come to be here in the first place?

Underlying this statement was the implication that the Indians belonged to the land, not vice versa, and that no justification was needed for their presence.[7] Harry insisted that current disputes between Aboriginal and non-Aboriginal peoples over land were flawed because people continued to avoid the issue of how these lands had been originally assigned. The answers, he explained, were contained in a story.

In a now familiar pattern, Harry sat upright, cleared his throat, and began telling the story. Once again Coyote loomed large. But much to my surprise, so did my first ancestor. The story featured a pair of twins charged to undertake a series of important tasks related to the creation of the earth and its first inhabitants. The elder twin performed his duties exactly as instructed, but the younger twin stole a written document—a "paper"—he had been warned not to touch. When confronted about his actions, he denied having done this. Because of this, he was immediately banished to a distant land across a large body of water. The elder twin was left in his place of origin.

The younger twin, Harry explained, was the original ancestor of white people; the elder twin was Coyote—"the Indians' forefather." "That's how come," Harry explained, "the Indians [were] here first before the white." He then stressed that "that's why the white man can tell a lie more than the Indian.... " Part of the deal struck with the younger twin (*my* first ancestor) at the time of his banishment was that his descendants would one day travel to the home of the elder twin's descendants to reveal the contents of the written document.

Time passed and all proceeded according to plan. The descendants of the elder twin multiplied and populated the North American continent while the descendants of the younger twin did the same in their designated homeland across the ocean. Eventually, after many years, the latter made their way to North America. But, things went badly astray when, true to their original character, the descendants of the younger twin began killing descendants of the elder twin and stealing their lands. They also concealed the contents of the "paper." When the conflicts between the two groups escalated, Coyote travelled to England to discuss ways of resolving these problems with the king of the younger twin's descendants. Harry recalled a segment of Coyote's speech to the king:

> Your children is coming.
> Lots of them.
> They come halfways already from the coast to the coast.
> And they don't do right to my children.
> Seems to me they're going to run over them.
> And they don't care much for them.
> Now we're going to straighten that up.
> And we're going to make a law.
> And the law that we're going to make
>   is going to be the law from the time we finish.

Together Coyote and the king produced a book that outlined a set of codes by which the two groups were supposed to live and interact. "When they finish that law," Harry explained, they call it the "Black and White" because "one of them was black and the other was white." They made four copies, three of which they agreed to distribute to the descendants of both groups.

Harry's sources for this story were able to trace the movement of the "Black and White" from England to various points in Canada. One man, TOH-ma, told Harry in 1917 that he had travelled with a man who was charged with delivering a copy of the "Black and White" to the legislature in Victoria. Another of Harry's acquaintances, Edward Bent, had gained access to the book. Having attended residential school, he could read English. But he died before he could reveal its contents to his colleagues.

By now I was very confused. This Coyote story had so little in common with the quaint and timeless mythological accounts in the published collections. I wondered about the references to my first ancestor. I had not encountered anything like this among the published accounts for this region. The Coyote at the centre of this story was not portrayed as the trickster/seducer/pest that he had been in the story Harry had recounted for us two years earlier. Rather, this original ancestor of the "Indians" was the obedient twin who dutifully followed the orders of his superior. In this story he represented goodness. My first ancestor, by way of contrast, represented the opposite: he was a liar and a thief. Even more surprising was Coyote's ability to travel freely between prehistorical and historical time zones as revealed in the segment of the story about the meeting between Coyote and the king. Such movement was uncommon in the early collections.

Because I had encountered so few references to whites and other postcontact details among the published "myths/legends" I had surveyed, I bracketed this story as an anomaly. The theoretical literature on the subject supported this move. For example, Claude Lévi-Strauss's *The Savage Mind*, one of the leading sources on myth at the time, had divided "myths/legends" into two separate zones—"cold" and "hot"—depending on their cultures of origin.[8] "Cold" zones were associated with Indigenous peoples with a mythic consciousness that tended to resist change; "hot" zones, on the other hand, were associated with Western peoples with a historical consciousness that thrived on constant, irreversible change. As Harry was immersed in a cultural zone which Lévi-Strauss would have classified as "cold," it followed that his corresponding narrative repertoire should be predominantly timeless and ahistorical.

But Harry's stories did not fit this pattern. Immediately after recounting his story about Coyote's origins and his meeting with the king of England, he proceeded to tell a series of four narratives situated squarely in the early twentieth century. Analyzed according to the Lévi-Straussian model, therefore, his repertoire was more "hot" than "cold." There was certainly nothing timeless about it.

Harry told the four historical narratives to illustrate the importance of the special power given to "Indians" via Coyote at the beginning of time. The first was about Susan Joseph, an Okanagan woman who had used this power to "doctor" a seriously injured man. The other three were about various individuals who had used it to cure themselves during times of crisis. Harry stressed that this power was intimately connected to the natural world:

> You got to, the kids, you know,
>   they got to meet the animal, you know, when they was little.
> Can be anytime 'til it's five years old to ten years old.
> He's supposed to meet animal or bird, or anything, you know.
> And this animal, whoever they meet, got to talk to 'em
>   and tell 'em what they should do.
> Later on, not right away.

I wondered why I had not encountered any such historical narratives among the early published collections that I had surveyed.

By September 1980, I was back again in Hedley. At Harry's urging I began to extend my visits. If I wanted to hear stories, he explained, I had to stay for more than just an afternoon:

> There's a lot of people come here just like you do.
> Some of them stay here two, three hours only.
> Well, I can't tell them nothing in two, three hours.
> Very little.
> But some people, one man, we talk, I and he, for over twelve hours.
> So they really come to know something of me.
> It takes a long time. I can't tell stories in a little while.
> Sometimes I might tell one stories and I might go too far in the one side like.
> Then I have to come back and go on the one side from the same way,
>   but on the one side, like.
> Kinda forget, you know. And it takes time....

He also warned me that if I were truly serious about his stories, I should not waste time: "I'm going to disappear and there'll be no more telling stories."

He was right about the value of longer visits. In addition to making time for more storytelling, extended visits enabled us to spend afternoons doing other things such as meandering through backroads at leisure, visiting people here and there, and running errands which served to prompt further memories and stories.

As always, Harry surprised me with his stories. He opened our first evening session in September 1980 with a long story about white newcomers. After establishing the story's setting at the junction of the Fraser and Thompson Rivers, Harry noted that it was a very old story that had taken place "shortly after when it's become real person instead of animal people" but before the arrival of whites. The focus was a young boy and his grandmother who had been abandoned by the rest of their community because of the boy's laziness. One day they were visited by an old man whom they invited to share a meal. This man taught them new and more effective methods of hunting and fishing in return for the gift of a patchwork blanket composed of the feathered hides of bluejays and magpies, which was all the boy and his grandmother had to offer.

Before departing, the visitor revealed that he was "God" in disguise and that one of his reasons for visiting them was to convey that "white-skinned" people would arrive someday to "live here for all time." He explained in detail how these newcomers would give the land a patchwork appearance with their "hayfields" and "gardens." But they would never take ownership of the land because "this island supposed to be for the Indians." God told the boy and the woman, "This is your place." As a testament to this statement, God placed the patchwork blanket on the ground, whereupon it transformed into stone. Harry explained that one of his lifelong goals was to travel to Lytton to find this important stone which had been concealed by an earlier generation to prevent discovery and possible theft by whites.

As with the earlier story about the twins, I decided to bracket this account. Although I had found numerous variants of the story among the old sources, the latter included no references to God or whites. Instead, the central figure was "Sun" or "Sun man" who gave the boy and his grandmother things like bows, arrows, and cooler weather.

I continued to visit Harry regularly throughout the rest of the fall. And Harry continued telling stories. After recounting the story about God's visit with the boy and his grandmother, he initiated a long cycle of Coyote stories. Again, God turned up in these stories. Having overseen the creation of the world and its first people, this "God" was always lingering in the background of the stories. Although Harry often referred to him as "God," he occasionally called him by other names. For example, in his story about how Coyote got his name, Harry used the term "Chief": "that supposed to be the Creator, or the Indians call him the Big Chief. Could be God in another way."

Harry's point was that this "Chief" had also endowed Coyote with both a name ("Shin-KLEEP") and special powers:

> I can give you power
>   and you can have power from me.
> Then you can go all over the place.
> You can walk everywhere....
> And there's a lot of danger,
>   a lot of bad animal and monster in the country
>   and I want you to get rid of that.

One of the stories was about Fox, who could revive Coyote from death. While some of the stories focussed on Coyote's good deeds, for example, his elimination of vicious cannibalistic monsters—*spatla*—who preyed on people, others highlighted Coyote's "prankster/seducer" tendencies, for example, his plot to snatch his daughter-in-law by enticing his son to climb to a world in the sky, thereby exiling him to another level of existence. His son eventually returned and sent his lecherous father running. Coyote had few restraints on his power until he encountered God (in disguise) whom he challenged to a duel. Annoyed by Coyote's hubris, God banished him to a remote place. "Just like he put him in jail," Harry noted. Harry ended his Coyote series with an expanded version of his story about Coyote's visit with the king of England. Except for the last story, all of these Coyote stories were firmly rooted in the deep prehistorical past—the time of the "animal people." (Harry called these "imbellable" stories. When I asked what he meant by "imbellable," he explained that when he asked for the English word for *chap-TEEK-whl*—the Okanagan term for stories from "way back" during the time of the animal people—someone had given him the word "unbelievable." Harry heard this as "imbellable" and applied it to his *chap-TEEK-whl* thereafter.)

At last I could see some tangible parallels between these stories and those that I had surveyed in the published records. However, just as I began to relax in this timeless zone of relative familiarity, Harry suddenly shifted back to the historical period. He told eight stories about *recent* human encounters with power. I wondered if he intended these to illustrate contemporary manifestations of Coyote's powers—they appeared to me as having much in common.

The first of these historical narratives was about foreknowledge. Just as God had forewarned a boy and an old woman about the transformation of the landscape by white agriculturalists, a man in the 1920s had forewarned his people about the alteration of the landscape by multiple highways. Another story was about powerful transformations in contemporary times. Just as Coyote transformed monsters such as Owl Woman to stone, so a group of Indian doctors, disturbed by the intrusion of the first trains through Sicamous, used their power to stop the train in its tracks. Just as Coyote and his colleagues had been endowed with special relationships with animals, so their descendants shared a similar relationship as revealed in the stories about hunters saved from death by wolverines and grizzly bears. Just as God had introduced the boy and his grandmother to easier means of procuring food, so a couple of cranes provided two hunters with similar skills. Just as Coyote could transform himself into whatever he wished, so could a man called "Lefty," who transformed himself into a wolf, a grizzly bear, and a frog to track a group of people who had abducted his sister. Just as there were monsters roaming around in Coyote's time, so too were monsters roaming through the landscape in more recent times, as evidenced in the story about a squirrel that turned himself into a "gorilla" and then picked up a boy and carried him on his shoulders from Hedley to Yakima.

By late 1980, Harry and I had established a lively written correspondence to fill in the gaps between our visits. Having been taught by a friend to read and write English, he enjoyed writing letters. Although the process of writing was always slow (it took several days and many jars of correction fluid to produce a short letter), Harry derived great satisfaction from it. He carefully filed all of his incoming letters so that he could re-read and savour them. In turn, I enjoyed receiving letters from Harry. "Oh say," he wrote on 7 February 1981, "I was going to tell you. I was verry Happy to hear from you. Last month you got here on 8th of January. When you left Im kind missin you Im still missin you tell I get a words from you that is why I was Happy than I get to started and writing letter." Once, he offered advice that showed his appreciation of good penmanship and a well-turned phrase. He advised me to write clearly so that he could decipher every word: "You write it so fast. Is not clear. Should do like I did clear to every shingle letter and clear. Can be much better. Better for me to read" (7 February 1981). Sometimes his letters were long: "I could not Help it for written a long letter," he wrote at one point, "because Im storyteller I always have Planty to say" (n.d.).

Harry included many personal reflections in his letters: "I can never forget for long time the good time we have when we together. Hope its going to be some more good times for you and I" (1 March 1981). Sometimes he advised me on issues of cultural protocol. Until around this time, I had been paying Harry standard consulting fees. In his letter of 7 February 1981, however, he suggested that I stop doing this. He was obviously uncomfortable with being "paid" for sharing stories: "Im willing to tell you a stories at any time. You don't have to pay me. If you happened to be around I might need your help or may not. Just depends." Likewise, I much preferred this new arrangement that enabled me to run errands with him in lieu of dealing in cash.

The winter of 1981 was a highpoint in our relationship as I had rented a cabin in the Coldwater Valley, south of Merritt, for the year. With only an hour and a half's drive from there to Hedley, we were able to get together regularly. In addition to visits at Hedley, Harry and I spent time at my Coldwater cabin. It was a busy year with lots of trips to see all his old friends throughout Nicola Valley, the Fraser Canyon, and Douglas Lake. In January and February, we travelled through northern Washington to take part in winter dances.

During this period, Harry opened my eyes to yet another new line of stories: historical narratives but with a strange twist. Each featured an extraordinary encounter with a lake monster, a devil, a strange snake, a talking cat, or another such being. According to folklore scholar Stith Thompson, such stories were common. And yet, they were rare in the published collections for British Columbia. I wondered if collectors, in their search for "authentic" mythological accounts, had glossed over such accounts because they were too Westernized.[9]

A number of these stories focussed on strange occurrences in and around lakes. For example, there were several stories about Palmer Lake. One involved a monster that swallowed a horse and released it a year later; another was about a herd of cattle that emerged from and then disappeared into the lake; and a third was about a man and his canoe swallowed by the lake. Okanagan Lake was the setting for a story about two men who disappeared mysteriously. And Omak Lake was the site of a number of strange happenings. One involved a blind calf that walked into the lake and never returned.

Other stories featured talking cats that could change at will into other forms. Some of these cats duped and killed nasty monsters or people who had insulted them. Others came to the rescue of those in need. For example, in one story, a cat used his power to endow a local man, Sammy, with cash. In another, a spotted cat warned a man against committing suicide. In still another, a cat took revenge on a woman who hated cats and treated them badly.

On concluding this series of stories, Harry took another sharp turn by recounting what he called "murder stories." Many of these were set in the nineteenth century: for example, the story of a woman named Madeleine, who murdered a white man who attacked her while she was travelling alone on the trail. Harry had been in touch with Madeleine until her death at ninety in 1918. Another featured a man named Joseph of Chopaka, who in the mid-1800s killed a white man suspected of surveying lands for whites. Another story involved a man named "Polutkin," who in 1845 was ordered by a chief to retrieve his wife who had deserted him for another man. There was also a story of Alexander Chilahitsa who took revenge on a man who had killed his wife while she was alone at their ranch; and another about Narcisse Tom Louis, who at the end of his life confessed to murdering a Chinese man. Few of these stories were straightforward accounts of conflict. For example, one story about George Jim, a local man who was captured, tried, and imprisoned in the 1880s, was more about the aftermath of a "murder" than the murder itself. According to Harry, Jim was abducted from the New Westminster Penitentiary midway through his sentence and taken to England where he served as an outlaw Indian in a sideshow. Harry also included numerous accounts of more recent "murders," many of which were still well-known and controversial.

Then, during the winter of 1982, Harry retold his story about the creation of the world and the first people. On hearing it again, I began to question my earlier reaction to it. Harry obviously considered it important enough to be told a second time. And it was, after all, the story that he claimed was missing at the political meetings of his youth—that is, the story that explained "how come Indians to be here in the first place." The story also explained why Indians and whites derived their power from two completely different sources. For Indians, power was located in their hearts and heads; for whites, it was located on paper. Harry elaborated again on the process required for Indians to gain power:

> Long time ago, the Indians just like a school.
> When they got to be bigger,
>   they send 'em out alone at night or even in the daytime.
> And left 'em someplace.
> Leave 'em there alone, by himself or herself.

It's got to be alone.
The animal can come to him or her and talk to 'em.
And tell 'em what he's going to do.
And that's their power.
They give 'em a power and tell 'em what they're going to do
    what work they going to do....
This power, they call it *shoo-MISH*.
That's his power.
That was the animal they talked to 'em.
Doesn't matter what kind of animal.
Any animal—bear or grizzly or wolf or coyote or deer—
    any animal can talk to 'em.

To illustrate this connection between the *shoo-MISH* and humans, Harry told another long series of stories. He began with the story of his wife, Matilda, who encountered a dead cow that gave her a song and told her, "You going to be a power women." He then told the story of another woman, Lala, who encountered a dead deer with a similar message and accompanying song.

Harry's story of Shash-AP-kin typified the stories in this cycle. Left alone at the age of ten or eleven by his father and a group of hunters, Shash-AP-kin began to play with a chipmunk. In an instant the chipmunk turned into a boy, who told him, "This stump ... you think it's a stump but it's my grandfather. He's very very old man.... He can talk to you [and] tell you what you going to be when you get to be middle-aged or more." At that moment the boy turned into an old man who told him that he would give him power to withstand bullets. He then sang a song and the boy joined him in the singing. The boy then fell asleep. When he awoke, "he knows already what he's going to be when he get to be a man." Harry says that when the white people arrived, "they all bad, you know. They mean. They tough." They shot Shash-AP-kin. But the latter was able to withstand their bullets by using this power he had received from the smooth stump. He lived to be an old man, Harry explained. "They never get him. They never kill him."

This last set of stories marked the end of our relaxed and easygoing visits. During the spring, Harry's health took a sharp downturn when a nagging leg ulcer required his hospitalization for six weeks in Penticton. It was a miserable time for Harry who had little faith in white doctors and their medicines at the best of times. Convinced that his ulcer had been caused by *plak*, a form of witchcraft, he believed that white doctors could not cure it. His view was that because a member of his community had triggered this ulcer problem in the first place, it would require an Indian doctor to heal it.

He found the hospital culture cold and alienating. Everything about it was antithetical to his ways—bedpans left standing in the washroom, windows locked in a closed position, enforced bedtimes, and so on. After six weeks, when he could stand it no longer, he checked himself out of the hospital on the grounds that it was "too dirty ... [and] no good for an Indian like me" (letter, 12 September 1982).

At home, he grew worse by the day. As he wrote on 27 September 1982, "Im really in Bad shape." As I was by then based in Vancouver, I urged him to consider a Vancouver-based Chinese herbalist. He was keen on this idea: "If I can only see that Chinese Doctor it don't mather much about the cost. Is to get Better. That's the mean thing" (letter, 27 September 1982). When the herbalist died partway through his treatments, Harry became thoroughly discouraged and depressed.

Throughout the next two years, he remained at home in Hedley where he tried to manage his ulcer on his own, supplemented by the occasional treatments by Indian doctors. He was happy to find a local Keremeos physician, a woman who was willing to work with his beliefs about the cultural source of his problems. I visited often, but our daily drill was very different from what it had been in earlier years. He now slept through most of the day and evening. Then he was awake and up all night, often moaning in pain. I made meals and drove him to his medical appointments. We resumed our storytelling sessions whenever he felt in the mood for them.

During a visit in mid-April 1984, Harry became so ill that he worried that his death was imminent: "Now I'm sure I'm not going to live any longer ... I could have died last night ... or maybe tonight. Never know." Nevertheless, he propped himself up, cleared his throat, and told a cycle of four stories. Each one was about an individual who could predict his/her own death. Although telling these stories sapped his energy, he seemed determined to get through them. I perceived that he had a larger motive in mind.

At the end of this cycle Harry sank back into his pillow and announced that "you can still hear that when I dead.... And that way in all these stories. You can hear that again on this (*points to the tape recorder*) once or twice or more." He continued,

> And think and look
>   and try and look ahead and look around at the stories.
> Then you can see the difference between the white and the Indian.
> But if I tell you, you may not understand.
> I try to tell you many times
> But I know you didn't got 'em....
> So hear these stories of the old times.
> And think about it.
> See what you can find something from that story....

He stressed again that he feared that he was approaching the end of his storytelling, "I'm not going to last very long."

So, take a listen to this (*points to my recorder*)
  a few times and think about it—to these stories
    and to what I tell you now.
Compare them.
See if you can see something more about it.
Kind of plain,
But it's pretty hard to tell you for you to know right now.
Takes time.
Then you will see.

He then stated, "That's all. No more stories. Do you understand?" Shocked and saddened, I replied, "Sort of."

It was a relief to hear that Harry had expected me to listen to his stories many times before drawing any conclusions. He stressed that they contained hidden messages and connections that would take time to decipher. I reflected on how passionately he had told his stories about whites and how quickly I had dismissed these as anomalies. Harry's comments suggested that he may have had more of a prior plan than I realized.

At this stage, however, there were more pressing concerns for all of us than analyzing the deeper meanings of his stories. Harry was growing weaker by the day. In desperation, he finally asked his neighbour, Carrie Allison, to call an ambulance. He was quickly admitted to the Princeton Hospital. After several months of treatment, he had improved enough to be discharged. But it was now clear to everyone that he was not well enough to live at home by himself. As he and Matilda had had no children, he was unable to draw on immediate family members for assistance. So he moved to Pine Acres Home, a seniors' residence operated by the Westbank Indian Band.

Institutionalized living, however, did not agree with him. Many of the residents were suffering from dementia so he could not carry on conversations with them. And he missed the familiarity of the Similkameen Valley. After a year, he transferred to Mountainview Manor, a seniors' complex located in the heart of Keremeos. He was happier there in a self-contained, ground-floor unit which felt more like home. His band also provided twenty-four hour home care which gave him a continuous sense of companionship and support. As with his earlier routine, he slept during most of the daytime hours and sat up all night. Worried about his digestive system, he ate almost nothing. I visited regularly and he continued to tell stories. But the old vigour and enthusiasm were diminishing.

There was one project during this period that kept his spirits high, however. In 1984 while he was living at Pine Acres Home, we began discussing the possibility of turning his stories into a book. He felt that the book should be widely disseminated throughout "all Province in Canada and United States, that is when it comes to be a Book" (letter, 27 January 1986). The project kept his mind occupied. And it also gave him a set of daily goals as he struggled to think of gaps. The best part was that it inspired him to tell more stories.

Many of these new stories focussed on his life history. He was very proud of his ranching experiences and wanted some of these to be included in the book: "I get to started feed stock from 2nd Jan. 1917 till 1972," he wrote on 15 May 1985. "50 years I feed cattle without missed a day in feeding season rain or shine. snowing or Blazirt. Sunday's. holirdays. funeral day. any other time ... 50 winter's that should worth to be on Book if is not too late."

Harry explained that he was twelve years old when he got his first paying job. It was with a crew of workers hired to thresh wheat and oats at Ashnola. He recalled every detail of the experience—driving the horses, cleaning up the straw, pushing all the grain into place, and piling it into baskets. Unfortunately, he hated it so much that he quit after a couple of months to try another job—pitching hay for fifty cents a day. When he quit the second job after just a few months, his mother, Arcell, took him aside, and scolded him for his poor work habits. She must have made an impact because he recalled that he took his next jobs as ranch hands much more seriously. The first of these was with family friend, Indian Edward, who gave him his first horse as payment for his work. Under Edward's tutelage, Harry quickly became a skilled horseman and cattle hand.

Harry spoke constantly of horses and their place in his early life. "Those days the horses was a big business because no tractor, no truck, no nothing but only team of horses. And saddle horse and wagon and buggy. Use the buggy to go to town, kinda fancy. Wagon, more like a tractor, trailer, something. Heavy work, hauling rails, hauling hay, hauling something heavy with the horses." Among his most poignant memories was the 1930s government campaign to exterminate the wild herds that roamed through the Similkameen.

He obtained his first ranch in December 1924, through his marriage to Matilda Johnny, a widow. Together Harry and Matilda established a good working relationship—buying, selling, and trading cows and horses. They bought and sold property until they had four large ranches between Chopaka and Ashnola. At one point, Harry employed a large crew to assist with his sixty horses and 150 head of cattle.

After Matilda's death in 1971, Harry cut his ranching operation back to fifty head of cattle. A nagging hip injury forced him to retire completely two years later. He sold all of his ranches and rented a bungalow owned by his longtime friends, Carrie and Slim Allison. The hip injury turned out to be a good thing for his storytelling. Although he had spent lots of time listening to his grandmother and her contemporaries tell stories, he did not begin to tell stories until he was immobilized by the injury. While running his ranches, he simply had no time to sit for hours telling stories. "When I get older," he explained, "and nothing I can do but tell stories." He explained that the stories all came back to him much like "pictures" going by.

Many of these dated back to his early childhood when he was left for long periods to assist his blind grandmother, Louise Newhmkin. Among the stories of her family history was a special one about her aunt from Brewster, Washington, who married a prominent white man, John P. Curr. Harry's grandmother adored this uncle whom she described as a highly respected "government man." Curr had lived with the Okanagan Indians for five years until his Okanagan wife died. Louise passed on many of Curr's stories to Harry. One of the most heart-rending stories chronicled the vigilante style murder of a prominent Similkameen chief by two members of Curr's brigade in the 1830s.[10]

By now I had assembled a representative sample of stories for the book. I had hoped that Harry would assist with this, but he declined: "That's really up to you," he wrote in a letter of 27 January 1986. "Don't have to ask me about it. I wrote the some of it or I mention on tape and you do the rest of the work. The stories is worked by Both of us you and I." I included Harry's story about the creation of the world and the twins as well as his account of God's visit to Lytton. Along with a selection of Coyote stories, I included a number of stories about early and more recent human encounters with their *shoo-MISH*. I concluded the volume with a selection of historical narratives dealing with Aboriginal interactions with whites. Unfortunately the publication process took more time than we expected. By 1987, Harry was worried that he might not live to see the release of the book: "Im in Hospital but I can't write.... We might see that Book yet I hope. Its all moste 2 years since we got start about that Book. Please let me know all you have know about for that Book" (letter, 8 March 1987).

Write It on Your Heart: The Epic World of an Okanagan Storyteller was finally released in late October 1989.[11] The timing was perfect. Harry was frail but able to study the book's contents. He was also well enough to attend the book launch celebration on 13 November in Keremeos. From his wheelchair, he was feted by a crowd of approximately one hundred friends and relatives, some of whom had come from distant points in Washington State. In addition to signing books, he made speeches, sang, and played his drum. In return, the local drumming group performed in his honour. This was his last formal outing. Harry died just over two months later on 25 January 1990.

Harry was very pleased with the book. His only concern was that it had not included all of his stories. I explained that we had recorded too many stories for one single volume and that presenting his words in poetic form had also

21

consumed extra space. With Harry's concerns in mind, however, I moved quickly to assemble a second volume of stories. Entitled *Nature Power: In the Spirit of an Okanagan Storyteller*,[12] it featured stories about human encounters with their *shoo-MISH*. Although I had not fully met Harry's objective to have all of his stories in print, I nevertheless felt the two volumes gave a representative sense of the whole.

Over the next few years, however, I continued to reflect on the stories that I had left out of these two volumes—stories such as Coyote's meeting with the king and others about talking cats and disappearing cows and horses. The latter were so unusual and so unlike anything in the Boasian collections that I had decided to put them aside. But then I began to wonder how much of Boas's editorial decisions had influenced my own selection process.

My timing for such questioning was ideal. In the early 1990s the Boasian research paradigm had become the subject of intense critical scrutiny.[13] The poststructuralist turn in the social sciences was partly responsible for this review. It had spawned a new generation of scholars intent on exposing the ideological foundations of anthropological practice. The Boasian project was an easy target. Critics such as James Clifford, Rosalind Morris, Michael Harkin, David Murray, and others focussed on a number of issues, in particular the Boasians' fixation on the deep past. Although the Boasians had recorded hundreds of Aboriginal oral narratives, they had limited themselves to a single genre: the so-called "legends," "folk-tales," and "myths" set in prehistorical times. They had little interest in the fact that many of their narrators were horsepackers, miners, cannery workers, missionary assistants, and laborers who maintained equally vibrant stories about their more recent past. As Harkin explained, the collectors' goal was to document "some overarching, static, ideal type of culture, detached from its pragmatic and socially positioned moorings among real people." Thus they "systematically suppressed … all evidence of history and change."[14] Such erasure had serious long term consequences for Aboriginal peoples.

Anthropologists working in South America were pursuing a similar line of argument at this time.[15] Their target was Claude Lévi-Strauss, who had used Amazonian examples to test his theories of "cold," mythic societies. As Terence Turner explained, "To base one's entire analysis of social consciousness … on one or a few traditional rituals and narratives and then to conclude that the culture as a whole is in the mythic phase, lacking a concept of history, may reflect a lack in the investigative procedure more than a lack in the culture."[16] Emilienne Ireland endorsed Turner with her study of "white man" stories of the Waura peoples of Brazil. She stressed that myth was important for its ability to "mak[e] statements about the present and the future." The Waura "myth," she explained, took "a historic tragedy of monstrous proportions and transformed it into an affirmation of their own moral values and of the destiny to survive as a people."[17]

Charles Hill-Tout, a British ethnographer who worked among the Okanagan in 1911, was particularly entrenched in the salvage paradigm. His position on the "mythology" he collected was that it was valuable for revealing "the mind of the native as it was before contact with white influence."[18] "In no other way now," he wrote, "can we get real and genuine glimpses of the forgotten past. They are our only reliable record.... "[19] Never mind that the "minds" in question were several generations removed from precontact times or that the tellers of the myths had not experienced life without whites.

The impact of this fixation on "myth" hit home one day when I was sifting through some fieldnotes sent to Franz Boas from British Columbia by his colleague, James Teit. Among the latter's notes was a version of the story Harry had told me about God's appearance at Lytton to trade his knowledge of whites for a patchwork blanket. According to Teit's account the visitor was "Sun" who traded four items—a gun, a bow, an arrow, and a goat-hair robe—for the old woman's "blankets of birds-skins."[20] Yet, when Boas edited the story for publication, he had removed the word "gun" from this list, thus transforming what may have been intended as a historical narrative into the more desirable "precontact" myth.[21] Boas was familiar with the story as he had recorded a Nlaka'pamux version at Lytton in 1888.[22] I was curious to see that just as Harry had told me that story during one of our first sessions, one of the Nlaka'pamux storytellers had similarly told it to Boas during his first session at Lytton.[23]

Such examples raised questions about the messages that collectors gleaned from their narrators' stories. Could Boas have mistaken a contemporary—even quasi-Christianized—story for a traditional "myth/legend"? Could he have edited a historical account to make it fit his vision of a prehistorical myth? And what about the Nlaka'pamux storytellers? Could they have selected this story for Boas, as Harry did in my case, to convey a political message—that whites were, and would always be, visitors on "Indian" land? Could they have told it to establish their superiority in relation to whites, that is, that they had had knowledge about the arrival of whites before their actual arrival? Did their "Sun" have associations with Harry's "God"? The Sun of the 1888 Lytton session was, after all, "a man" who lived in the sky above an "ocean" somewhere far to the east.

Determined to resolve some of these issues, I scoured the old collections hoping to find further references to guns, whites, and other such things. Although Boas was preoccupied with suppressing such "impurities,"[24] I knew that one of his most active field associates, James Teit, was not. Teit was fully immersed in the contemporary lives and languages of Aboriginal peoples through his Nlaka'pamux wife, Antko, and his work as a translator for the Aboriginal political protest organizations.[25] Through such cultural immersion, he was more aware than many of his colleagues of the full range of stories in their natural settings.

I quickly found a little-known Teit collection featuring seven stories literally peppered with cultural "impurities."[26] It was exactly what I needed. Even better, these were Similkameen stories. They were published as "Thompson Indian Tales," but this was in fact an error. Teit's fieldnotes had indicated clearly that some of the stories had originated with "Bert Allison," a prominent Similkameen chief.[27]

The opening story was perfect. Entitled "Coyote and the Paper," it featured an encounter between "Old One or Great Chief" and Coyote in which the former tried to replace Coyote's excrement (from whom Coyote often sought counsel) with paper so that Coyote would have an easier time carrying it around. Coyote accepted the paper but then lost it a few days later. The narrator considered this a major loss. "If Coyote had not lost it [the paper]," he explained, "the Indians would now know writing, and the whites would not have had the opportunity to obtain written language."[28] In the context of this story, Harry's accounts of the twins and the paper, and others about meetings between Coyote and the king were not so unusual after all.

There were references to whites scattered throughout this collection. Several stories featured groups of young men—brothers/companions—who travelled to "towns" in search for work: blacksmithing, carpentry, farmwork, cowboying, and splitting wood. Life was not easy as they had to deal with nasty employers and landowners who made impossible demands on them. For example, in one story, a boy named Jack encountered a man who so objected to his marriage to his daughter that he threatened to kill him if he could not clear a dense piece of forest in a single day, or if he could not make water flow instantly from a distant creek to his house.[29]

Several stories targeted white authority figures. In one account, a young man, Jack, was challenged by his employer to steal the priest from the next village. So he concocted a grand plan. He dressed himself up as a priest, went to the church in the next village, lit the candles, and began to perform mass. When the resident priest saw this, he knelt down and prayed. Jack told him that God had sent him to tell the priest that he was so pleased with his work that he wanted him to go to heaven without dying. All he had to do to get to "heaven tonight" was to climb into a sack and allow himself to be carried to a designated spot. The priest did as he was told. Jack then carried the sack to his uncle's place. Once there, he told the priest that when he heard "the cock crowing, [he would] know that heaven is near, and [he would thus] be taken up soon after that." When the people arrived the next day, they found the priest in the sack crying, "Let me be! The cocks have crowed and I will soon ascend to God." On realizing that it was all a trick, the priest returned home.[30]

I could see many connections to Harry's stories. But what interested me most about this collection was its 1937 publication date. Since this was fifteen years after Teit's death, I deduced that these were stories that Boas had withheld from publication due to their "impurities." He must have changed his mind toward the end of his career because he assigned Lucy Kramer to the task of editing the stories for publication in the *Journal of Folklore*.[31]

These little-known Okanagan stories provided a rich historical context for Harry's stories. Finally there was tangible evidence that Harry's forebears were not strictly "mythtellers" locked in their prehistorical past. I was now keen to look more closely at how Teit had handled the issue of individual variation in his earlier publications. His 1917 presentation of three Okanagan creation stories offered some valuable insights on this. Instead of following the usual pattern of turning the three stories into one composite story, Teit presented each story on its own.[32] The end result was a set of three very different perspectives on how the world and its first peoples came into being. The first, entitled "Old One," explained creation as follows:

> Old-One, or Chief, made the earth out of a woman, and said she would be the mother of all the people.... Old-One, after transforming her, took some of her flesh and rolled it into balls, as people do with mud and clay. These he transformed into beings of the ancient world.... (80)

The second story, told by a Similkameen narrator, offered a different view:

> The Chief above made the earth.... He created the animals. At last he made a man, who, however, was also a wolf. From this man's tail he made a woman. These were the first people. They were called "Tai'en" by the old people, who knew the story well, and they were the ancestors of all the Indians. (84)

Later, "Old-One" made "Indians" in much the same way. He blew on them "and they became alive." Teit noted that this story evolved into "the story of the Garden of Eden and the fall of man nearly in the same way as given in the Bible."

The third story, entitled "Origin of the Earth and People," had some obvious links to the first one, but it was still quite different from the other two:

> The Chief (or God) made seven worlds, of which the earth is the central one. Maybe the first priests of white people told us this, but some of us believe it now.... Perhaps in the beginning the earth was a woman.... He transformed her into the earth we live on, and he made the first Indians out of her flesh (which is the soil). Thus the first Indians were made by him from balls of red earth or mud.... Other races were made from soil of different colours.... (84)

An Okanagan creation story published in 1938 by anthropologist Leslie Spier shed more light on the issue of individual variation. Collected by L. V. W. Walters, one of five students in Spier's anthropological field school, the story was attributed to Suszen Timentwa, chief of the Kartar Band. Like Harry's origin story, Timentwa's story included references to whites, books, and laws. "[I]n the beginning as in the Bible," explained Timentwa, "God created the world, and created animals." This God gave Coyote a "little book" that he explained would "get you help to watch you from today."[33]

Like Teit's second account above, Timentwa included Adam and Eve in his story:

> After Adam and Eve did wrong, God took away one land from the top and put it to one side for the Indians-to-be. God took the laws with the Indian land and left the other land without laws. Then God built an ocean to separate these lands: one land was for the Indians, another for the white people. Indians did not need books because they knew things in their minds that they learned from the creatures. About the time of Christ, God made the creatures. This was before Christ was born, so that Christ could preach about the other land.... When the white people came to the Indians here, the priest told the Indians what they had forgotten. (177)

It was difficult to determine a common storyline among these stories.

A survey of neighbouring Nlaka'pamux creation stories collected by Teit revealed a similar range of diversity. According to one, "Old One" took some soil from an upper world, formed it into a ball, and threw it into a lake. On hitting the surface of the water, it shattered and became "a broken mass of flats, hollows, hills and islets" much as we see now.[34] According to another, Earth was a woman who lived with Stars, Moon, and Sun long before the world was formed. Because of her constant pestering, Sun abandoned her. Eventually, Stars and Moon did the same. "Old One" then took pity on her by transforming her into the present earth who gave birth to "people, who were very similar in form to ourselves." But they knew nothing until "Old One" travelled around teaching them things.[35]

An elderly "shaman ... from Sulus" told Teit that his grandfather had told him that "Old One" descended on a cloud from an upper world to a large lake. He pulled five hairs from his head and threw them onto the surface of the lake, at which point they became five "perfect" women who were endowed with "speech, sight, and hearing." He asked each what they would like to be in life. The first said she would like to be "bad and foolish, and ... seek after my own pleasure." She claimed that her relatives would "fight, lie, steal, murder and commit adultery. They will be wicked." The second wished to be good and virtuous and have children who would be "wise, peaceful, honest, truthful and chaste." The third wanted to be the "earth" upon which her sisters lived. The fourth wanted to be "fire." And the fifth wanted to be "water," from which people drew "life and wisdom." He then transformed them. The third daughter "fell backwards, spread out her legs, and rolled off

26

from the cloud into the lake, where she took the form of the earth we live on." The children of two of the women were male and female. They married "and from them all people are descended." According to yet another account, "Old One" encountered a woman who was alone and very unhappy about her situation. To make her happy, "Old One" transformed her into "the earth, which he made expand, and shape itself into valleys, mountains, and plains." Her blood dried up and became "gold, copper and other metals." Then "Old One" moved on to "make the Nicola country." He then created "four men and a woman," (some thought "four women") who became the first inhabitants. After teaching them how to survive, he left. But before doing so, he promised to return at which point "your mother, the Earth, from whom all things grow will again assume her original and natural form."[36]

The collections were just as divided on the subject of Coyote. In fact, Teit recorded so many varied Okanagan perspectives on Coyote that he added a note to highlight this point:

> Some think Coyote belonged to the earth, like other people. He was an Indian, but of greater knowledge and power than the others. Some think he was one of the semi-human ancients. Others think he did not belong to this world, but to some other sphere, such as the sky or spirit-land. Still others think he was a kind of deity or chief, or helper of the Chief, before he came to earth. In the opinion of some Indians, Coyote acted with a purpose, and knew that he had been sent to fulfill a mission. Others think he did not know, but that his actions were prompted by some other power, and that he did not transform the monsters or perform other acts for the purpose of benefiting mankind. All agree that he was selected for the mission he performed; but whether he was living in the sky when selected, or on the earth, or elsewhere, is not certain.[37]

Teit's emphasis on cultural fluidity, however, was offset by others' efforts to draw hard conclusions. Hill-Tout, for example, had claimed in 1911 that Coyote was "not a native product of the mythology of the stock" at all, but rather adopted from elsewhere.[38] Heister Dean Guie, a newspaper journalist, concluded that Coyote was better understood as a children's storybook character. With this in view, he edited and sanitized a collection of adult stories collected by Christine Quintasket. In the process, Guie turned Coyote into a generic "Imitator/Trick Person"—a fairy tale figure of sorts—who rarely acted in truly offensive ways. The book sold well. But Coyote suffered badly in the process.[39]

Viewed against this backdrop, Harry's stories assumed much greater significance. His account of the twins, for example, was now one of a series of diverse creation stories maintained by his people over a long period.

Similarly, his account of Coyote's meeting with the king of England was just as distinctive a version as numerous others. Harry's historical narratives—about unusual employees who turned up to work in local ranches—were part of an established genre of stories set in towns, farms, and ranches and featuring all sorts of people in search of jobs as blacksmiths, farmworkers, and carpenters. That Harry's stories of white/Aboriginal conflict had few parallels in the early collections did not mean that his predecessors had not told such stories. Early collectors simply did not have any interest in them.

Comments by both Teit and Boas revealed that Aboriginal peoples were extremely eager to exchange stories about contemporary political issues. In 1916, Teit explained that his success as a salvage ethnographer depended on listening to stories about local political issues:

> For many years back when engaged among the tribes in ethnological work for American and of late for the Canadian government, the Indians almost everywhere would bring up questions of their grievances concerning their title, reserves, hunting and fishing rights, policies of Agents and missionaries, dances, potlatches, education, etc. etc. and although I had nothing to do with these matters they invariably wanted to discuss them with me or get me to help them, and to please them and thus to better facilitate my research work I had to listen and given them some advice or information."[40]

Although he assisted the chiefs in disseminating their contemporary histories, in political contexts, he was unable to incorporate these into his ethnographic collections.[41]

Boas also noted in his field diaries and letters that many of his interviewees were eager to engage him in discussions about current issues. A Squamish chief, for example, saw Boas's interview session as an opportunity to air some of his current political concerns:

> "Who sent you here?" "I have come to see the Indians and to tell the White people about them." "Do you come from the Queen's Country?" "No, I come from another country." "Will you go to the Queen's Country?" "Perhaps." "Good, when you get there go to the Queen and tell her this. Now write down what I say: Three men came [i.e., the Indian agent and two commissioners] and made treaties with us and said this is the Queen's land. That has made our hearts sad and we are angry at the three men. But the Queen does not know this. We are not angry at her."[42]

Little of this sort of discussion made its way into his publications. Boas also noted inconsistencies among storytellers and often worried that many were telling him nothing but "nonsense."[43] Comments on this issue from his assistant, George Hunt, did not help: "You know as well as I do," he wrote to Boas, "that you or me can't find two Indians tell a storie alike."[44]

In all of this I could see the potential for a new Harry Robinson volume highlighting the breadth of his stories. Whether they were old (i.e., "myths" about Coyote and others) or new (i.e., stories about recent murders or floods) was not of great concern to Harry. What mattered most to him was "living by stories." He wanted to show the cultural importance of maintaining a full range of stories. If people—whites and "Indians"—knew that stumps could turn into chipmunks and that chipmunks could turn into "grandfathers," they would cultivate a very different relationship to the land. If they knew about people like George Jim of Ashnola who had been wrongly abducted from the New Westminster prison in 1887, and Tom Shiweelkin who was wrongly killed by an early brigade of whites, they would carry a different view of their history. Knowing about large birds that could carry humans, lake creatures that could swallow horses, and grizzly bears that could shelter travellers in distress would show people that the world around them consisted of many different forms and layers of life.

Through disseminating such narratives, Harry was promoting an awareness that would generate more storytelling. That others told these stories with different twists and turns was not a concern. In fact, Harry often incorporated their twists into his own stories. And although he would never tamper with storylines or fictionalize any part of a story, he incorporated seemingly extraneous details where he felt they belonged. For example, when he learned that whites had landed on the moon, Harry immediately incorporated this detail into his story about Coyote's son's trip to and from an upper world.

While assembling the first two volumes, I had not appreciated the full scope of Harry's perspective on storytelling. Along with several generations of scholars and others, I had been seduced by the Boasian paradigm which reified the mythological past and promoted the stereotype of the "mythteller"—the bearer of the single, communal accounts rooted in the deep past. Harry's stories about Coyote's meeting with the king and others about cats, cows, horses, and everyday animals doing supernatural things did not fit this model. But no amount of editing would make a "mythteller"[45] of Harry Robinson. He would have been insulted had the label been applied to him. He was a storyteller in the broadest sense of the term.

Harry had stressed in 1984 that he was "going to disappear and there will be no more telling stories." At the time, I assumed that he was referring to the demise of his stories. However, when I re-listened to this comment, I realized that I had missed his point. He perceived his death as a blow to the process of storytelling. He had worked hard over the years to ensure its well being. In the 1970s he had painstakingly adapted all of his stories in English to accommodate a growing number of listeners who spoke little or no Okanagan. Through the 1980s he had submitted these English versions of his stories to audio tape so that they could carry on without him. He had also spent afternoons in his local band office telling stories in his Okanagan language. His final move was to release his oral stories in book form so that they would reach a broad audience "in all Province in Canada and United States" (letter, 27 January 1986).

Living by Stories brings Harry's objective closer to fruition. And once again, Coyote looms large. The way Harry put it, everything hinged on the book produced by Coyote and the king. Although he never read its contents, he knew the story about it and that was what mattered. He would pass the story on through his own book. And its message would be clear to all: that whites were a banished people who colonized this country through fraudulence associated with an assigned form of power and knowledge which had been literally alienated from its original inhabitants.

NOTES

1. Two members of our party, Randy Bouchard and Dorothy Kennedy, knew Harry well. They had notified him in advance of our visit. The third member was Michael M'Gonigle.

2. Paul Radin, *The Trickster: A Study in American Indian Mythology* (New York: Schoeken Books, 1956); Gary Snyder, *The Old Ways* (San Francisco: City Lights Books, 1977); and Barry Lopez, *Giving Birth to Thunder, Sleeping with His Daughter, Coyote Builds North America* (New York: Avon Books, 1977).

3. James A. Teit, Marian K. Gould, Livingston Farrand, and Herbert J. Spinden, in *Folktales of Salishan and Sahaptin Tribes*, ed. Franz Boas (New York: Stechert & Co., 1917); Charles Hill-Tout, "Report on the Ethnology of the Okanaken of British Columbia, an Interior Division of the Salish Stock," in *Journal of the Royal Anthropological Institute* 41 (1911): 130–161 (reprinted in Ralph Maud, ed., *The Salish People: The Local Contribution of Charles Hill-Tout, Volume 1: The Thompson and the Okanagan* [Vancouver: Talonbooks, 1978], 131–159); and Leslie Spier, ed. (with Walter Cline, Rachel S. Commons, May Mandelbaum, Richard H. Post, and L. V. W. Walters), *The Sinkaietk or Southern Okanagon of Washington* (Menasha, Wisconsin: George Banta Publishing Co., 1938).

4. Mourning Dove, *Coyote Stories* (Caldwell, Idaho: Caxton Publishers, 1933; reprint, Jay Miller, ed., Lincoln: University of Nebraska Press, 1990).

5. Franz Boas, *Indianische Sagen von der Nord-Pacifischen Küste Amerikas* (Berlin: A. Asher & Co., 1895); for a recent English translation of this work, see Randy Bouchard and Dorothy Kennedy, eds., *Indian Myths & Legends from the North Pacific Coast of America* (Vancouver: Talonbooks, 2002); James A. Teit, *Traditions of the Thompson River Indians of British Columbia* (Boston: Houghton, Mifflin & Co., 1898); and id., "Mythology of the Thompson Indians," vol. 8, part 2 (New York: American Museum of Natural History, 1912), 199–416.

6. Teit, *Traditions*, 28. The Latin segment appears in footnote 73 on p. 105.

7. I am grateful to Lynne Jorgesen for this comment.

8. Claude Lévi-Strauss, *The Savage Mind* (Chicago: University of Chicago Press, 1966).

9. Stith Thompson, *The Folktale* (Berkeley: University of California Press, 1977), 9.

10. A quick survey of the historical records uncovered nothing about John P. Curr. Historian Richard Mackie concluded on the basis of the pack train, the men with uniforms, the mention of a few white men living here and there, and the execution of the chief that the setting for this story was probably circa 1858–62. He noted that it seemed typical of "the American overland militaristic migration to the Fraser or Cariboo gold rushes." Mackie explained that the chief would not have had a letter from Ottawa before 1871; however, he could well have had such a letter from a surveyor or a government employee from Victoria or New Westminster by then. He dated it at 1858–59 (e-mail correspondence, 1 August 2005). Historian Dan Marshall offered a similar view. He suggested that Curr's brigade may have consisted of miners. "Starting in 1858," he explained, "large companies of miners, many of them old Indian fighters, took the Columbia-Okanagan route to the BC goldfields. These companies ranged in size, many of them amounting to hundreds. The number of deaths that occurred on either side of the border during that year suggests that 1858 may be the time period in question, references to Ottawa and Vancouver aside" (e-mail correspondence, 5 August 2005).

11. Vancouver and Penticton: Talonbooks and Theytus Books, 1989.

12. Vancouver: Douglas & McIntyre, 1992; reprint, Vancouver: Talonbooks, 2004.

13. See, for example the following: James Clifford, *The Predicament of Culture: Twentieth-Century Ethnography, Literature, and Art* (Cambridge: Harvard University Press, 1988); David Murray, *Forked Tongues: Speech, Writing and Representation in North American Indian Texts* (Bloomington: Indiana University Press, 1991); Michael Harkin, "Past Presence: Conceptions of History in Northwest Coast Studies," *Arctic Anthropology* 33, no. 2 (1996): 1–15; Judith Berman, "'The Culture As It Appears to the Indian Himself': Boas, George Hunt, and the Methods of Ethnography," in George W. Stocking, Jr., *'Volksgeist' As Method and Ethic: Essays on Boasian Ethnography and the German Anthropological Tradition* (Madison: University of Wisconsin Press, 1996), 215–256; Rosalind Morris, *New Worlds from Fragments: Film Ethnography, and the Representation of Northwest Coast Cultures* (Boulder: Westview Press, 1994).

14. Michael Harkin, "(Dis)pleasures of the Text: Boasian Ethnology on the Central Northwest Coast," in *Gateways: Exploring the Legacy of the Jesup North Pacific Expedition, 1897–1902*, eds. Igor Krupnik and William W. Fitzhugh (Washington: Smithsonian Institution, 2001), 93–105.

15. Jonathan D. Hill, ed., *Rethinking History and Myth: Indigenous South American Perspectives on the Past* (Chicago: University of Illinois Press, 1988).

16. Terence Turner, "Ethno-Ethnohistory: Myth and History in Native South American Representations of Contact with Western Society," in *Rethinking History and Myth*, ed. Jonathan D. Hill, 174.

17. Emilienne Ireland, "Cerebral Savage: The Whiteman as Symbol of Cleverness and Savagery in Waura Myth," in *Rethinking History and Myth*, 172. In British Columbia, anthropologists Julie Cruikshank and Robin Ridington were drawing attention to similar issues. See Julie Cruikshank, *Life Lived Like a Story: Life Stories of Three Yukon Elders* (Lincoln: University of Nebraska Press, 1990) and id., "Images of Society in Klondike Gold Rush Narratives: Skookum Jim and the Discovery of Gold," *Ethnohistory* 39, no. 1 (1992): 20–41. See also Robin Ridington, *Trail to Heaven: Knowledge and Narrative in a Northern Native Community* (Vancouver: Douglas & McIntyre, 1988) and id., *Little Bit Know Something: Stories in a Language of Anthropology* (Iowa: University of Iowa Press, 1990).

18. Hill-Tout, in Maud, *The Salish People, Vol. 1*, 137.

19. Ibid., 149.

20. James A. Teit, New York City: Fieldnotes, Anthropology Archives, American Museum of Natural History (AMNH).

21. Teit et al., *Folk-tales of Salishan and Sahaptin Tribes*, 34.

22. Boas, *Indianische Sagen*, 52.

23. Ronald Rohner, ed., *The Ethnography of Franz Boas: Letters and Diaries of Franz Boas Written on the Northwest Coast from 1886–1931* (Chicago: University of Chicago Press, 1969), 99–100. For a more detailed examination of this story, see Wendy Wickwire, "Prophecy at Lytton," in *Voices from Four Directions: Contemporary Translations of the Native Literatures of North America*, ed. Brian Swann (Lincoln: University of Nebraska Press, 2004), 134–170.

24. For more on this, see Judith Berman, "The Culture As It Appears to the Indian Himself." See also Charles Briggs and Richard Bauman, "'The Foundation of All Future Researches': Franz Boas, George Hunt, Native American Texts, and the Construction of Modernity," *American Quarterly* 51, no. 3 (1999): 479–527.

25. For more on James Teit's political activism, see Wendy Wickwire, "'We Shall Drink from the Stream and So Shall You': James A.Teit and Native Resistance in British Columbia, 1908–22," *Canadian Historical Review* 79, no. 2 (1998): 199–236.

32

26. Teit, "More Thompson Indian Tales," *Journal of American Folklore* 50, no. 196 (1937): 173–190.

27. Teit, Philadelphia: Fieldnotes, American Philosophical Society (APS).

28. Teit, "More Thompson Indian Tales," 170.

29. Ibid., 180.

30. Ibid., 184.

31. Ibid., 173. Footnote 1 explains that "the following hitherto unpublished tales have been taken from manuscripts by the late James A. Teit and edited by Lucy Kramer."

32. Teit et al., *Folk-tales of Salishan and Sahaptin Tribes*, 80–84.

33. Spier et al., *The Sinkaietk*, 197–198.

34. Teit, *Mythology of the Thompson Indians*, 320.

35. Ibid., 321.

36. Ibid., 323–324.

37. Teit et al., *Folk-tales of Salishan and Sahaptin Tribes*, 82.

38. Hill-Tout, in Maud, *The Salish People, Vol. 1*, 134.

39. Mourning Dove, *Coyote Stories*. See also Alanna K. Brown, "The Evolution of Mourning Dove's Coyote Stories," *Studies in American Indian Literatures* 4, nos. 2 & 3 (1992): 161–179. A new collection of stories recorded by Darwin Hanna and Mamie Henry—*Our Tellings: Interior Salish Stories of the Nlha7kapmx People* (Vancouver: UBC Press, 1995)—helped to reverse this trend. Herb Manuel's presentation of Coyote was never static or abstract. In fact, Manuel described Coyote so vividly that one would think that he had met Coyote: "He was kind of always undernourished. He was, in human flesh, a skinny, tall man with drawn-in cheeks [who] ... spoke with a drawn-in voice. He spoke funny. You knew it was him when you heard his voice" (32).

40. National Archives, RG10, vol. 7781, file 27150-3-3, Teit to Duncan Campbell Scott, 2 March 1916.

41. One notable document, a "Memorial to Laurier," presented by the Interior chiefs to Prime Minister Wilfred Laurier at Kamloops in 1910, was a history of the nineteenth century from the perspectives of the chiefs. For more on this, see Wickwire, "James A.Teit and Native Resistance," 1998.

42. Rohner, *The Ethnography of Franz Boas*, 86.

43. Ibid., 38.

44. Ibid., 239.

45. British Columbia poet Robert Bringhurst has recently introduced the term "mythteller" to the British Columbia anthropological lexicon. Based on his study of the Haida oral narrative collections of Boasian ethnographer John Swanton, Bringhurst concluded that the storytellers were "mythtellers." See *A Story As Sharp As a Knife: The Classical Haida Mythtellers and Their World* (Vancouver: Douglas & McIntyre, 1999).

A *SPATLA* WAS KILLED BY RABBIT AND CHIPMUNK

Eliminating spatla *was no easy task.*

I could tell that stories, three, four days
  and never end.
But I can't tell 'em all now.
Just a part of it, just the first part.

The Indians, they know, just like they do in the Bible says.
They know the same way almost,
  not exactly the same way, but likely.

And these woman, Indian,
  they say there's four of them.
Women.
Big one.
Extra big.
And they call that *spatla* in our language.
But I cannot say what it would be called in English.
But only in my language, they call 'em *spatla*.
They are bad.
They packs that basket and they got the babies—
  the two-year-old or more, or little baby,
    and throw 'em in that basket.
Then they kill 'em by that cactus.
Then they take 'em in the bush and cook 'em and eat 'em.
They make a fire, and they roast 'em.
They roast 'em on the stick,
  get 'em cooked, and eat.
They might eat the whole baby at one meal.
Then they look for another one for the next meal.
That's what the *spatla* do.
They eat person.
They eat people.
Not the big one, but the small one.

They like the baby ones, because they tender.
Just like little deer.

And the chance they will get,
  it will eat the big person if they can only kill 'em.
Well, they can kill 'em.
They easy to kill because him, herself, they're big.
They do anything to the other person like we are.
They kill 'em and eat 'em.
But they like the smaller one more than they do the big one,
  or the big person.
That's the stories in Indian.

And in the Bible, that these two man,
  they're big too.
They alike and they sound the same way.
And these stories in Indian—*spatla*,
  the white people, they must've heard that from some Indian
    somehow in Omak maybe long time ago.

And one time, at the rodeo time,
  that was about the 1980 or '81, one of these years,
    I was there.
And I see the white people,
  they make a show, like that *spatla*.
Just how it was told for the stories.
One man, they make some kind of pack.
The other one make the two, three of 'em, maybe four.
And they packed a great big thing, you know,
  but it's not heavy.
They light but it looks like a heavy pack.
And they walks around in the ring,
  on the outside the ring,
    the way to go into a grandstand.
And they go around, the two of them.
That shows, they do that when they imbellable* stories.
The white man did that, not the Indians.

---

* This term refers to *chap-TEEK-whl*—the Okanagan word for stories from "way back"
during the time of the "animal-people." When Harry asked for an English translation of
chap-TEEK-whl, someone gave him the word "unbelievable." Harry heard this as
"imbellable" and applied it to his *chap-TEEK-whl* thereafter.

The white man can do.
Not the Indian.
But that was the stories
  they know that from the Indian.
And they figure they do the same, but not exactly.

And a lot of people, white and Indian,
  they don't know what that is
    when they see these mans around.
They only say,

        "My, they're a big mans too.
        And they got a big pack."

That's all they knew because they couldn't see.
And I did see.
But I knew that's *spatla*.
That's like the way they look like when he was there
  between Konkonala and Loomis
    in that little valley.

And I seen the place,
  that little lake where they got killed.
That *spatla* with the pack on.
Well, whoever killed 'em,
  they were just an awful little little person.

Rabbit and Chipmunk, they small.
They couldn't kill the big animal like that.
But they did—they killed 'em.
That's way, way back.

So that's the stories.
I was wondering if anybody could remember
  that time, that rodeo in 1980 or '81,
    when these two man,
      they had a great big pack
        and they goes around on the road, like,
          when you go into a grandstand.
Go playing around, two, three times walk that way.
And everybody seen 'em.
And everybody thinks they big, tall man.
And they got the big pack too.

Why?
They don't know why.
They don't know anything about it,
  white people and Indian.
I'm one of the Indian but I know what's about.
That's *spatla.*
That's the way it looked like when he was 'round,
  way, way back.
The white people, they heard that from the Indian somehow—
  the part of the stories, a little,
And they make show for that.
See?
That'll be all for the first few story.

One of these *spatla,* they called 'em,
  that's supposed to be a woman.
There're four of them.
The other three was killed by the Indian somehow,
  but I cannot remember how it came by this moment.
But later on, if I had a lot of time,
  I could think a little
    and I will know who killed 'em and how it's killed.
But I can't say that right now.

But one of them was killed by Rabbit and Chipmunk.
He was killed between Loomis and Konkonala.
In that, that little valley.
I go by on the horseback.
And I see that little lake, the small little lake.
That's where they kill 'em.
A long, long time.
That's one of 'em.
And the other two was killed by the Indian somehow
  but I cannot say because I don't remember.

But the other one, like the second one,
  Coyote—he killed that.
Coyote, he met that woman, big woman—*spatla.*
And as soon as he met 'em,
  Coyote, he knows this was a bad woman.
She's a person-eater.

Person-killer, eater.
And they're afraid
  he might kill him and eat 'em.
So, the first thing they do, they make a friend with them.
They try to make a good friend with that woman.
So finally the woman they think that all right.
This is a good man, they can be my friend.
So they tell her that he do too.
He kill the person and eat 'em, just like she do.
Just tell that lie to her
  just so they think they can be friend with 'em.

So, anyway, that way.
And Coyote, they got a chance to kill her.
And he tell a lot of lie
  and tell her,

      "We can build a big fire.
      We can carry a lot of wood, and pile 'em.
      And we can bring some, a lot of, stone
        and put them on the pile of wood—the stone.
      And we can start the fire on that pile,
        and it will be a big fire.
      And then we can dance, we can sing this song.
      Then I got the drum and I beat the drum.
      And then we can dance right around the fire,
        you and I.
      Because we doing the same things, the both of us.
      Today we met and we make a good friend.
      And we can go together.
      Then we can hunt for person to kill 'em
        so we'll have something to eat
          at any time.
      That is why we're going to have a kind of powwow
        around the fire.
      We're going to have a dance.
      But it's got to be big fire with stones on it.
      And let the stone get hot, get red hot.
      Then we dance. I beat the drum
        and we go right around the fire and dance."

So they do that.
They buy a lot of wood
  and they carry a lot of big stones.
They big enough to carry.
And they put 'em on that pile of wood.
And they start the fire.
When that fire get good and started,
  and was a big fire,
    and they sing the song
      and beat the drum.
And him and her, they hook their arms together, like.
When they dance around the fire,
  and the woman was close to the fire, like.
And Coyote was—the woman between him and the fire.
So he's got a good brains to figure it, Coyote was.
And he dance around and dance and dance.
And finally they get kind of dizzy a little
  because they going around fast.
And he push the woman to the fire.
And they got some stick already with the fork.
They cut the sticks with fork.
And they had 'em lay there, two of them.
And this woman says,

      "What are you going to have that stick for?"

      "Well," he said,
      "When the fire gets go down, we take that stick—
          you can take one and I take one—"

He only need one, but he make one extra,
  just so he could tell her,

      "You could take one and I take one.
          And then we get the fire together with that stick.
          Leave 'em there."

But he knew he was going to use it not that way.
But he's going to use it in different way.
But the woman didn't.
She didn't know.
When they was pushed by Coyote to the fire,

and Coyote, they got that stick there,
  and put 'em right on the neck, you know,
    and hold 'em there.
Then they get burned to death.
Killed 'em that a way.
That's one of the *spatla*.

And the other one was killed by Chipmunk and Rabbit.
But the other two was killed by the Indians
  but I don't remember.
I did know.
But by now, just for this moment, I cannot say.
I kind of forget,
  but I will remember later on.

  Wendy: How was the one killed by Chipmunk and Rabbit?

That's the one, the Rabbit and Chipmunk killed.
That is the one.
They killed her with that pack on.

  Wendy: How did they do it?

They do the same.
They build a fire, but dig a hole.
Dig a hole about two feet deep
  and they build, pile a bunch of dry wood,
    in the bottom of hole.
And then they put some stones on top of this wood.
Because Rabbit is white
  and Chipmunk is kind of a yellow colour.
And *spatla* was kind of a dark blue, more like our colour.
And, in those days they were an animal.
But that was supposed to be—that's how the Indians become.

And they met *spatla*.
And *spatla*, they wanted to know,
  how come for Rabbit to be white,
    white as the snow.
She wanted to be like that.
She wanted to be white.
But it wasn't white.

But the Rabbit was white.
Just like snow.

Ask Rabbit,

> "How come for you to be white?"

> "Well," Rabbit, he says,
> "I use some certain stuff, to use,
>   so I can be white.
> And that's what I'm going to do.
> Chipmunk, see, he's not white.
> I keep her, but later on I fix 'em up
>   and then he'll be white like me."

So *spatla* says,

> "Why you didn't do that work on me first
>   —before her?
> I wanted to be white."

Rabbit said,

> "All right.
> If you don't mind, I and her,
>   we can make you to be white right now."

Said,

> "All right. Do it."

> "Okay."

She can't see the straw.

Says,

> "All right. You dig a hole for us."

And *spatla*, they used her finger
  to dig a hole.
They can dig a hole with her hand.
Dig a hole about two, three feet deep.
A long hole, because is tall.
So it can be fit in that hole.

Because she got to lay there.
So they make that long,
  'bout six feet or more—eight feet, maybe.
And they makes that hole
  and they said to 'em,

> "Get us some wood and break 'em
>   and pile 'em in the bottom of the hole."

And *spatla* did.
Because she can do it.
She's strong.
When they get the work all done,
  tell 'em to get stone and put stone on top of the wood.

Spatla did.
Pile the stone on top of the wood.
That's right in the cut, right in the hole.
When they get that done,
  and Rabbit, they start the fire.
When that fire, and fire comes out of hole,
  when they gets good and hot,
    good and burn, and rock will all turn to be red,
      from fire.
And he tells *spatla*,

> "It might hurt a little, but not too bad.
>   We have to tie you with the rope
>   and we can throw you in there.
>   And then you'll be there
>   and we tell you to turn over.
>   You can turn over, you can turn over that way.
>   You can roll right over.
>   'Til the fire gets quietened down
>   and we'll tell you, all right, you get up.
>   You get up then.
>   You get up, and you'll be white.
>   Only ways to get you to be white."

That's what they tell 'em.
But they wouldn't live that long.
  because they trying to kill 'em that way.

But that's the way they tell 'em.
All right.
Spatla did all that work.
When they get them done, and they start the fire,
  they all standing there and watch
    'til it gets to be very good big fire.
And they tie her, with the rope they put her arms like that,
  and tie 'em on their body
    and tie 'em right to his leg.
And they moved 'em and then they pushed and pushed 'em
  'til they gets to the edge of the hole.
And they just slide 'em in.
And they fall on the top of these red-hot rocks
  on his back.
They slide 'em in and they drop.
His back was against the rock.
And they got burned from the hot rock and the fire.
And they couldn't move
  because their arms was tied onto his body.
And their legs is all tied.
And they couldn't put their legs like that.
They was tied good and tight.

And they hurt.
They said they really hurt.

> "Turn me over."

And they said,

> "Tough enough.
>   Lie for a while."

And Rabbit said little while
  because they got to turn to be white.
And little while, and they getting pretty low on his
  breathe.
And then he get that fork stick,
  and they turn 'em.
Soon as they turn 'em, his heart's getting to the rock.
No more.
They killed 'em that way.

The big woman, strong woman.
But Rabbit and Chipmunk, they are small.
But they killed a big person.
They killed 'em that way.

That's between Loomis and Konkonala.
Not far from road.
Was a little lake is still there today.
I go by there on the saddle horse.
  and I turn off and I take a good look.
I did see where the *spatla* was killed.
But I can't say when.
It is way, way back.
So, that's the end.
That's all I can say about it.

You Going to Get Married to Coyote's Son

Coyote's son is betrothed to a "woman"
who is not what she appears to be.

The next stories,
  that's another Coyote.

That's another young Coyote.
Not the same one … goes up to the moon.
That's not him.
This is another one.
But still, it was Old Coyote's son.
And that's supposed to be younger
  than the one that goes up to the moon.
This is another one,
  but it's Coyote's son.

He got—the Indians at that time—
  long time,
    they had the camp at one place.
That could be down,
  down towards Spokane somewhere.
That way
  where they get the white camas.
That's down in the Wilbur, I think, the little town, its name was.
Wilbur, just the other side of Grand Coulee.
The next town from Grand Coulee in the flat country, that way.
That's where they getting the white camas.
Even today they get them from that area over there.
And that story could be around in that area.

And the Indians they were staying in one camp, the bunch of 'em.
Not only a few, but a bunch of 'em.
They had a camp.
And, these Indians, they went out.

Only the womans.
And they went out and get that camas,
  that white camas.
They dug 'em, you know.
They got the sharp stick, and hard,
 the old bushes of the saskatoon bush.
They're hard wood.
They sharpen them and then when they dig,
  you know the camas was so deep in the ground,
    about four inch.
They got to dig it, you know.
And that's what the womans do.
They go out, the bunch of 'em.
And then they dig this camas all day, and then they come back.
The next day they went out again.
They got the season, only, for that.
Maybe they could dig that for only two weeks.
Maybe three weeks.
And no more.
They out of season,
  they getting old, and no more.
So they got to do that every day, you know,
  to have lots of 'em.

So while they were there camping,
  and there's some mans,
    and these mans, they goes out hunting, you know.
They get a deer
 or birds,
    antelope, or something like that, you know.
Groundhog.
That's what the mans do.
They goes out hunting.
But the womans, they dig this camas.
And even the little girls, you know,
  they go along too because they teach 'em, you know,
    how to dig.
And they had a camp and they had a teepee.
And you know how the teepee is.
We seen 'em in this picture here, a while ago.
And they high.

And they is open up there, that's where the smoke comes out.
But it's high.
So, they had those, you know.
They had the teepee but smoke out to the top.
The teepee, it's smoking up.
But it's open up there.
But it's high.

And, the four of these girls,
  all sisters, the four of them.
And, that's the ... they call that the monsters,
  these girls, the four of them.
They not young, they kind of old, you know,
  they middle age.
They were together, the four of them.
And they say,

> "We can go and see this Indian camp, at night.
> We can go over there and see 'em."

They know.
They understand.
Coyote, he is the chief in that camp.
He was there.
And he's got a son.
His son was a pretty-looking man.
A single man.
And these girls, they say,

> "We could go over there and see 'em.
> Maybe we take that Coyote's son."

That's one of them could be her husband.
They figure.
So they all go together.
And they come to the camp at night.
And all the Indians, they all in the tent, you know,
  in the teepee.
Getting dark, like now.
Nobody outside.
All inside.
And these four girls, they come outside.

And they stand there.
And they said, the one of them,
　he said,

　　　"You see if you going to see somebody in there."

And they stand, and they kind of dance, you know.
They up and down.
Up and down.
Up they goes.
And higher and higher
　and higher and higher.
And they was so tall
　and they could look into the teepee.
The teepee up to the top where it's open.
Where the smoke comes out.
They raise up, by doing it, you know.
See, that's his power.
Her power.
Then they was that high.
And they looked, they reached,
　they looked in there
　　and then they see the people.
But these people, they don't see them,
　they don't know they're up there.
See, they're not up there but only his head up there.
They were so tall.
Still standing on the ground.

And they look, and the Coyote,
　they know that was Coyote.
The Old Coyote.
And another one alongside of him.
Just young.
That's his son.

All right.
These ladies, they come back, and same thing.
Down and down
　and down and down and—
They come to ordinary.
And then they says to the other one,

"All right. You go see."

And see, this stories, it's hard to believe.

He says to the other one,

    "You go see."

And the other one,
  they just up and down again,
    just like that.
They right up,
  right up,
    right up.
And then they look.
And they see 'em.
The whole four of 'em.
They do that
  and every one of 'em,
    they seen 'em.

That's Coyote's son all right.
And they says to their sister,
  that was the youngest one,
    they told her,

      "You the one that going to get married to Coyote's son.
        Tomorrow night, or next night,
          we can all come,
            but you can come,
              you can change into a person
              and you can just go in there.
        And you can just walk over there
          and sit down alongside of Coyote's son.
        And nobody will say anything.
        And that's going to be your husband.
        And we go away."

So they do that.
The next night, they all go
  and these other three they were standing a little ways.
And the younger sister she come
  and change herself into ordinary person, you know.

They a young girl.
They walked in.
And they just walked and sat down alongside of Coyote's son.
And, she says,

> "I come.
>> I come to marry you.
>> I'm going to be—
>>> you're my husband."

All right.
Everybody satisfied.
That was okay.
But they don't know where this young girl come from.
They don't know who she was
  and where she come from.
They don't know that.
But they don't seems to wanted to know.
Because that was made by their power.
So they wouldn't think that way.
They just have to let 'em go.
All right.

These other three, they go away.
Nobody seen them.
They went away.
So this young lady that was stay there a few days,
  and they says,
    they says,

> "I better go.
>> Go along with this digger that dig there,
>>> white camas."

> "Oh sure, you can go because all the ladies,
>> they all go and they dig.
>> You can go."

All right.
They make up the stick, you know, so they could dig the camas.
So they went along with these others.
So they make that,
  they're good friend.

That's a new friend.
All the new sister-in-law, something like that, you know.
They like it.
But they's a monster.
· That's the *spatla*, they call.
And that's the same one,
  he turns into owl.
And that's the one I was telling you a while ago.
They was a big person,
  a big man or a big woman.
But they turns into owl.
That's the bunch.
That's the same one.
They supposed to get four of them.

So they goes along with the diggers every day.
Then, when they get out quite a ways
  away from camp and they dig,
    and not too long, a little while,
      and they go away.
        go away a little ways,
          a little more,
            a little more.
Pretty soon, they go out of the sight,
  all by herself.
Nobody with her, just her alone.
And they get out of the sight.
Maybe a little hill and they go around the hill.
They go over the hill.
So nobody could see.
But night come, you know, by the time is going to go home,
  when she come back and they got lots of them.
By God, she must've been good digger.
The other ladies, they got little bunch, you know,
  about that much in the bags.
But she got lots of 'em.
By God, that new friend,
  they can sure dig!
They dig good.
So they like it.

So finally, when they at the camp,
  and they got the open fire inside the teepee, you know,
    and they cook.
You know, the ladies, they cook.
And this new friend, they do some cooking there.
And sometimes they might burn her finger.
From picking up something hot.
And then they got scared like they hurt.
And they kind of jump.

> "*Hoh!*"

They could say that.

> "*Hoh!*"

That's a word they never heard.
They don't know what that means.
Most of the time, every time they got kind of scared
  or got burned on the finger,
    then they said,

> "*Hoh!*
> *Hoh!*"

So the old people, they say,

> "What's the matter?
>   That's a different word.
>   We never heard that word.
>   They don't sounds good."

And that lady, they always go by herself,
  alone when they go way out.
And they always come back with a big bags of white camas.

> "Maybe we should watch.
>   Might be monster."

So they pick up the good man, strong man
  and tell 'em,

> "Tomorrow, when the ladies goes over there,

and then you go behind
  and you sneak.
Don't let them see you.
You can watch them from the distance.
You stick out,
  you peek out.
If she goes by herself, alone,
  then they goes on the other side,
    and you guys can sneak around,
      and you watch from the distance.
You might find out what she was."

All right.
They all go and they were together a little while,
  then she goes a little way, little way.
Pretty soon they go all by herself.
Went out of the sight.
And these boys, they go round on one side and watch.
She never see these boys.
Watch 'em.
When they get to the ...
  nobody there—
    then the same way, they stand.
Stand and go like that.
They do that.
And pretty soon, they grow up
  and they could see the tall woman,
    big one.
And they got the long arms.
And the finger were sharp.
And instead of use that stick,
  they just dig that with her hand.
And bring the dirt right over.
And pick 'em up.
In the first place, they went out
  and look where they were digging.
And they could see,
  don't looks like they digging with a stick.
Looks like they digging with something else, you know.
They damage the ground quite a bit.
That what they seen first.

Some of these womans, one day they might go the one direction.
And go out of the sight.
And next day, from where they was,
  they go to some other direction.
And these other ladies, they go over there
  to where she was before,
    the day before.
And they could see that.
Looks like they don't use that stick.
They told the other people,
  that's why they watch 'em.
And they could see.
They was a tall and big one.
And when they come back and they tell the other people,

> "That's the monster all right.
> That's *spatla*.
> He raise up and they tall."

Yeah, they got scared.
They thought,

> "One of these days, they going to kill us.
> Only herself.
> They going to kill all of us.
> Maybe we should go away."

The next time they go,
  these ladies went out and dig.
She always go alone and they always go by herself,
Out of sight.

> "You watch 'em,
>   as soon as they go out of the sight,
>   all you come back.
>   And when you get here, we pick up
>   and pack the stuff
>   and away we go.
>   And she can be out there 'til night come.
>   And then come home.
>   There'll be nobody here.
>   We going to leave."

So they do that.
They just watch 'em 'til they goes out of the sight.
On the other side of the hill.
These other ladies, they all go back to the camp
   and pick up the things and pack 'em
      and away they go.
And the old Coyote, old Coyote, he said,

> "I'm not going.
>   I'm going to stay right here
>   'til she comes back."

Because old Coyote, he's supposed to—
   that was his job.
He's supposed to kill the things like that.
That's what he always do.
So he says,

> "I'm going to stay here.
>   'Til she comes back and see what we'll do."

He figures he's going to kill her.
Or her could kill him.
One or the other.
All right.

The rest of the people, they go away.
And Coyote was around.
And then Coyote use his power.
And the night come and this lady,
   they goes back to her friend.
They not there, they gone.
Well, she thinks,

> "Maybe they go ahead of them.
>   I'll go home."

And she coming.
They come to the camp.
Nobody.
Looks like they take everything,
   and pack 'em and go away.
But they could see like the garbage

or anything that's kind of rotten
    or something,
        they put them together.
They could see that on the ground.
And they went over there and take a look.
And they kind of dig.
And there's a lot of worms.
All worms, the worms was so big, you know.
Lots of 'em.
And she thinks,

> "This is Coyote.
> They change himself into worms.
> That's Coyote.
> I'm going to smash 'em all."

So, herself, soon as they missed the people
    and they changed herself into *spatla* again.
A big one.
And Coyote, they know.
And they went down there
    and they going to bite 'em.
        with his mouth, you know.
They lay there with her head like that.
And Coyote says,

> "Here, here, here.
> Don't, don't, don't.
> Don't chew me.
> I'm going to spoil your teeth if you do."

So then they got scared.

> "I guess I'm going to spoil my teeth if I chew that."

So they thinks,

> "I'm going to look 'round for some stick or something,
>   and I'll just hammer 'em and smash 'em."

So they went out and look around for something else.
Coyote get up and go.
And then, Coyote was running.

And he run up to catch 'em,
  to kill 'em,
    but Coyote is gone.
But they catch up to his son.
The one that was his wife, you know.
He went away, but he stop.
Waiting for his dad.
So Old Coyote, they caught up to his son.
And they told his son,

> "Your wife is a monster.
>   That's a *spatla*.
>   I got away.
>   But you watch out, he's coming."

So, Coyote, they turn and go to some direction,
  but this young Coyote,
    he run.
And his wife coming.
And he see them.
And, he missed the Old Coyote.
But they see that that was her husband.
All right.

> "I'm going to caught up to him
>   and I'm going to eat 'em."

So they run up.
They couldn't catch 'em.
The young Coyote was fast, running.
He run for a long ways and he get tired.
And he think, well, he got tired,
  this one is going to caught up to him.
And they going to kill him.
And little while, they could see somebody ahead of him.
He was a man.
Sitting right in the open,
  right on the ground.
He was sitting there
  and his leg was like that.
And then he sitting, you know.
And then he play.

"Oy, oy, ex ko bah.
Eh ba ba."

That's how come now, when they play the stick game,
  they do that.
You seen the stick game player?
They do that.
That's the way.
That's the bone.
That's supposed to be a man sitting there.
But that's *Bone.*
That's the stick game—*Bone.*

And he sing that song.
And young Coyote come, and he hear them,
  and he says to him,

> "Could you help me?
>   This monster was coming,
>   they going to kill me."

> "Well," he says,
> "I'll see what I can do for you."

That's all.
And then he still play.

> *"Oy, oy, ex ko bah.*
>   *Eh ba ba."*

All right.
And the young Coyote was worried, you know,
  because his wife was gettin' closer.
When she get there, they goin' to be killed.
And he says to this old man,

> "You better make it snappy and see what you can do for me,
>   I'm going to be killed."

And this old man say, he said,

> "All right. I'll see what I can do for you."

And Coyote says,

"Well, better do it. She's gettin' close."

So this woman gettin' pretty close.

And this man, that's the *Bone*,
  he says, to young Coyote,

"All right, come here."

And young Coyote get there and he hold him.
And they hold him
  and he hold him like this and he still sing his song.
And they put 'em like that.
And he talk to him and he says,

"I'm gonna throw you. And you can go on the air.
  and you can be on the air. I throw you.
And you gonna go long ways.
Then you hit the ground.
You landed on the ground.
When you landed on the ground, which way you going,
You just landed on the ground, you just run ahead that way.
Not too far you can see a teepee. Somebody live there.
And you can see one woman live outside the teepee, they
  sittin' outside.
And that's my sister.
You can come to her.
And when you get to her, then you tell her,
  'I sent you from here to her.'
Then you tell your trouble and she can help you.
I don't know what's she's going to do for you—
  but she can do something some way.
To save you."

All right.
He still hold him like that.
Then, he said,

"All right."

Then he throw him.
And young Coyote went on the air just like a bullet.
Long ways.

And they landed on the ground.
And he run straight ahead.
And he see the teepee.
And the woman was sittin' outside a little ways from the teepee.
And this man, the one that throw 'em,
After they throw him, the monster come.
They figure they see he was gone.
But they thought they goin' to kill this one.
So they went and grab 'em.
They thought they goin' to grab 'em.
And down they went to grab 'em.
And *Bone* he's way over there, they still singin' his song.
By God, they run over there and they gonna grab 'em
And they lay right on 'em.
Bone they jumped way over to one side.
And they do that for a long time.
They wasting a lot of time that way.
By God, that monster, they say,

    "The heck with him, I couldn't get him."

So they beat 'em.
They go a little ways.
And this man they sing, sing his song louder and louder.
And by God that monster they get mad and come back again.
Says,

    "This time I'm going to get 'em."

When they come, they try to get 'em but they couldn't catch him.
Still sittin'.
They jump while they still sitting.
And he landed ...

    "*Oy, oy, ex ko bah,*
    Eh ba ba ... "

That means they don't care for that monster.
Just like the hair on his leg, you know.
They figure just like that.
Don't care.

Monster, they really mad.

And they went away.
Away and come back.
Wasting a lot of time.

Finally they thought, the heck with them,
  and they go.

But this boy, he landed there and he run and see this woman.
And he told 'em about it.

Well, this woman says,

      "All right."

Says to the boy,

      "I'll tell you.
        You just young. But I'm old.
        I'm way older than you.
        But when she come, I can kill her.
        But you going to be my husband if you don't mind that way
          because I'm old.
        But you only young.
        But in another way if you don't like it that way, she's going
          to kill you.
        She will kill you.
        But when they comes, I kill 'em.
        But you and I go together.
        You gonna be my husband."

Well, that boy was scared, you know, to die.

      "All right, that will be okay."

So they had that,
  when they make the arrowhead,
    for arrowhead, you know, the tip of, just little pieces.
But they sharp, just when you broke the glasses,
  bottles ... little pieces, they sharp.
Something like that.
They chip off when they make the arrowhead.
They had a bunch of that.
And they get that and then they put 'em on top of her head.

Put them there.
Then, when that monster come, they just scrapin'.
And then they see 'em from here and this woman tell 'em,

> "You can come and kill me if you want.
> I'm not gonna run.
> I stay right here."

And he says to that man,

> "You stay there. Don't run.
> Stay behind me. She'll come and get me first."

This monster come and kind of lays on that woman.
They thought they gonna bite 'em on the head.
This woman, she seems to go under them.
They got the belly ...
They cut 'em open.
Split 'em open.
And then they came out all the insides.
And they went over there and then that monster he got another heart.
His heart is here, but she got another one on the top of her head.

And he squeeze that right on the top of her head.
Squeeze 'em and smash them.
Pull 'em out.
Kill 'em.

So that's the end of that stories.
They got the man all right and then they were together.
So they kill that monster.

They don't seems to be right.
But that's the way it goes.
So we finish this.

Now here's another story ...

COYOTE MAKES A DEAL WITH THE KING OF ENGLAND

God calls on Coyote to perform a very important task.

For a long time, Coyote was there
  on the water, sitting on that boat.
And he eat right there.
And then they got a fire.
And the fire, they never go out.
They still burnin' just like it was when they first set the fire.
It's that way all the time.
And, been there a long time, just like they put him in jail.
They still there.

And for many years.
And the white people came from east
  and they kept moving to the west coast.
That's likely in California, in that area.
All along the west coast.
And the white people, they got a boat.
And they go on the boat like from San Francisco.
And they go across the sea to Australia.
Or, they go to China.
Go to New Zealand on the boat.
They always do that for a long time.

And one time, they see somebody on the water.
They could see somebody.
Looks like somebody was sitting on the boat.
There was smoke. They got a fire.
And they wanted to get closer.
They wanted to know what that was.
Looks like a person.

So they drive the boat closer but they never can get close.
Just about the same distance at all time.

They follow them around and around.
And they couldn't get close.

So they leave it.

And they get on the other side, that's in Australia
  and they told the people there about it.
And they come back and they seen him again on the way back comin'.
And they told that man.
They figure out how they gonna get closer.
So finally they put on the special boat.
Just a bunch of man in there, just a special boat.
They just look for that.
They can go out if they see 'em.
That boat supposed to go very fast.
Special.
And they want them to get closer.
When they get closer, they can keep comin' and they can get picture.
Then when they get closer, they want to know what that was.
Who?
What is it?
Looks like a person.
The little boat's got a little shack there.
Never see that before.

So they went out in that special boat.
And finally they see him again for quite a ways.
And they run to it.
And it looks like they're gettin' closer but no more.
They just about the same distance all the time.
And they follow 'em around.
Go for a long ways and maybe circle and ...
  chasin' him around for a long time.
And the fog come.
The fog on the lake ... and they disappeared.
And they don't see 'em.

So they go back.

Another time.
There was quite a few times they went after him.
They changed the boat and they put on a better boat.

Faster.
So they want to get closer and take the picture.
Or they can take him if they can.
They want to get him.
They see him again and chase him around.
They couldn't get any closer.
Just so far and that's about all.
No matter how fast they go,
   they get away from that just the same.

So they couldn't make it.
Then chase him around and there'll be fog.
And that's the time to lose him.

So finally they give up.
They don't seem him no more.
When they see him, they always chase him.
But when they can't see him, what they gonna do?
No more.

And that's for a long time.
They try to find.
They don't find him no more.
So finally, another time, after that,
   after they was chased around by white people,
      long time after that,
         God sent the Angel to Coyote.
Sent the Angel.

Do you know what the Angel was?
Do you know?
The Angel, God's Angel, you know.
They sent that to Coyote.
And Angel flew and get to Coyote.
And he see that he was still there.
But the white man couldn't find him.
And told Coyote,

            "God says at one time you work for him.
               You walked all over the place.
               But he put you here on the water.
               You going to be here until the end of the world.

Just before the end of the world, he's going to let you go out.
And then you going to go on the same place again.
But you got be on last time.
But now God sent me here to hire you again,
  just for short time.
Not going to be like it was before.
Not for long time.
Just for a while to give you the power.
Then you going to do the work again."

Coyote said,

"All right, whatever he says I will."

"All right,"

Angel told 'em,

"You got to go on the water.
All around.
And you can go right to England.
When you landed to England and you come to the edge of
  the water
    with your boat, that boat you are on there,
      you can go on there.
When you come there, get off, and you can drag your boat
  out on the dry ground
    so they wouldn't float.
Right in the open.
Nobody can see that boat.
And from there you can walk to where that king is.
You just go over there.
And nobody will see you.
And you can come to see the king.
And you can talk to the king,
  and you and the king going to make the law
    [for] the white people and the Indian.
That's what you going to do.
God wants you to do that.
Then they give you power so you can do whatever they
  want for you to do."

Coyote said,

> "Okay, I go."

Well, he's got to go because they wouldn't say no.
So, Angel left him.
And then he went from there.
They must have go through by Panama, but nobody know.
Then they go on the Atlantic.
Then they get to England.
Then in the beach, you know, where there's nobody, hardly any people,
  that's where they landed.
Then he come into dry land
  and he drag the boat even more so they wouldn't slide.
Then they walked to where the king is.
And there's a lot of people.
Big town.
And the king, they got a lot of people all around watchin' him.
Watch where nobody can go near.
No stranger, nothing.
Gotta be another governor to get to the king.
But not no stranger or anybody.
Lots of soldiers watching.
And Coyote went through there.
Nobody seen 'em.
And he come to the king's place, king's house.
And he come to the door.
And of course, he got some cooks there.
Somebody has to do the cooking so the king can be eating, you know,
  just like we do here.
So they come to the kitchen door.
They knocked on the door.
And the cook, they run and open the door.
And they see this man.
Jump.
Kinda scared.
Told him,

> "Don't scared."

Just okay.

They look different.
Looks like Coyote but it looks like a man.
Just kinda half-and-half.
So Coyote told 'em,

> "King, he's here."

> "Yeah, he's in the room there."

> "You go over there and tell him you seen me.
> I am another king. I am another king.
> You tell him,
> > 'There's another king that was standing there at the door.
> > They want to see you.'
> Then you come back and I go.
> And I want to see him.
> I want to talk to him."

So, this cook, they run back, see the king and told him,

> "There is a man standing there.
> Funny-looking man.
> He says he was a king.
> He's coming to see you.
> He wanted to talk to you."

And the king, he never thought about who's watchin' him.
They never think about it.
They never thought to report that stranger.
They never think about it.

Only thing he says,

> "All right, tell him to come."

But there's a lot of people watching him.
They should report who's watching
  so they can get him away or kill him.
They never thought about that
  because God's thought.
Then all he says is,

> "Tell him to come."

And the cook came back and told him,

> "All right, you go."

They go in there.
They walk to him and shake hands.
And he says to the king,

> "I'm another king. I come to see you.
> I want you, you and I, we can talk business.
> And we going to make a law.
> Because you king and I king."

He says to the king,

> "All your children, they went from here
>   and they get across into my place, into my country.
> Then from there they go east, they go west,
>   and they went about halfways already.
> And they don't do good with my children.
> So that's how I come here to see you
>   so we can make a law and then so our children they can
>   be good.
> Not to be in trouble, not to be bad to one another.
> That's what I want to do."

And the king says,

> "Well, what did my children do for your children?
> What did they do? Try to kill 'em or what did they do?"

Well, Coyote said,

> "They just don't care for them.
> They just go and claim the land
>   and they just do as they like.
> If my children tell them, 'Here, this is mine,'
>   then they will kill 'em.
> But my children, they just got to be scared.
> In another way, they just figure they can kill the Indian.
> So that's not good.
> Shouldn't be that way.

Should be good to one another.
And that's what I come here for."

And the king, they not satisfied.
Finally, they says to Coyote,

> "That word that you tell me, that's not right.
> Your word, it sounds like war.
> Sounds like war.
> If you are king and I am king, we should fight.
> Put up a war.
> Sounds like the way you talk."

Coyote says,

> "Yeah, it kinda sound that way."

But he says,

> "I can tell you one more thing.
> I want you to get up and walk to the window
>   and get to the window
>   and you can look out through the window.
> And stood there awhile and see what you can see outside.
> You can see through the window.
> Then you come back and sit down again.
> Then you could see we put up a war, we fight.
> All right.
> We'll do that.
> But when you come back and get on your chair,
>   if you say, 'No, we not going to fight,
>   we not going to have a war,'
>   that's another okay.
> But we can mark that down on the paper so it can be that way
> for the rest of time to the end of the world."

Because that's God's thought, you know.
And the king no more to say.
They let him go to the window.
And look through the window for a little while.
And they could see plain,
  there's all kinds of Indian.

They're thick as could be.
Nothing but Indian.
They all had feather on their head.
And they all had a spear on the sharp end.
Handlebar so big.
They all had that and there's nothing but Indians.
And where is the people they supposed to be watching for him?
And then they never see these bunch of Indian.
That's Coyote's power.
That's the power that God give him to come to see the king.
If there's anything that happens like that, they can use his power
  because God want 'em to, whatever Coyote says, it can be that way.

King look at him and by God, there's a lot of Indians.
He turns around and sat down and never said nothing for a little while.
Coyote told him,

> "Well, what do you think? Say something.
>   Whether we're going to have a war or not,
>   it's going to be really up to you."

King says to Coyote,

> "I think we not going to have a war because you all ready.
>   Your soldiers are all here.
>   But I am not ready.
>   Take me quite a while to get ready, but you ready.
>   So it's no use.
>   I can't step out and make a war when I am not ready.
>   But you are ready."

And Coyote told 'em,

> "Did you say no?"

> "Yeah."

> "But that's going to be your word from now 'til the end of
>   the word.
>   We'll never fight.
>   Once you say that, we'll never fight."

And that's the second time it was told by God,
  when they jump over the slough.
Was told not to fight.
First.
And this is second time.
And he said,

    "No, we not going to fight."

Then Coyote remind him,

    "This is the second time.
      Once you say that we not going to fight,
        we can make out a paper and sign."

Then he told him, Coyote says to him,

    "You remember, I am the one that your children chased me
      around on the sea.
    Way down.
    This is the one.
    They want to get close to me
      so they can take my picture.
    Or they can take me.
    That's what they figure. But this is me.
    Now, if you got a camera, pick up your camera
      and take all the picture
        you can take out of me before we could talk the business,
          before we can sign the paper. Get your camera."

The king get up and get the camera and took picture of Coyote
  sitting or standing or walking.
Take picture.
When they finish taking picture of Coyote,
  Coyote told 'em certain word,

    "You write it down.
      You write it down just the points, like.
      But when I leave you, then you can do the rest,
        take your time and do the rest.
      When you finish, all the paper, that could be the Indian law,

you give 'em to my children.
Not right away, but long time from now."

So, that's the settlement that they make.

And Coyote told 'em,

"What we should do, you sent your children into my country
and tell my children how big land they want.
And they could find how big did they want in each bunch.
Then your children will be surveyed just what they want.
And that's going to be Indian reserve.
We call that Indian reserve.
But that just for the Indians to be in there, not to be crowded
by your children.
This line, white people can go to the line and stop right there.
Not to go into the reserve.
But they can use the rest, the outside of the reserve
but they could leave the Indians alone right in reserve there
to be free.
You put that down and you sent your children.
They are the ones that are going to survey."

About they all told him,

"You write it all down.
Then it can be that way 'til the end of the world.
And this reserve it can be written down reserve.
Reserve at all time.
Can never be sold.
Can never be changed.
Can be trade.
That's all.
Can be trade.
Can be surveyor, surveyor.
Can be trade, but never can be sold.
Never can take away from Indians.
But still the Indians, they got a right
on the outside of the reserve as well."

So the king, they not really satisfied for this.
But they just got to do it,

But was kinda force by Coyote
  because they seen that Coyote's soldiers.
And go over that word again.
While they were seeing that soldiers, all Indians, and Coyote told 'em,

> "If you say, 'No, we not going to have a war,'"

Coyote says,

> "All right, that is if you say 'all right, we'll have a war,'
> All right we *will* have a war. I can let them know.
> And they'll come in,
> And they'll be the one that going to kill first.
> They'll kill you first before your children here.
> We'll have a war right here."

So, just to scare.
And that's why he's not satisfied.
Just to scare 'em.
And was just forced, like.
Coyote just force 'em to do something he don't really like.
And that idea is still the same right now.
They white people, they still not really satisfied.
But still they couldn't get the reserve away from the Indian.
They couldn't buy 'em. They not supposed to be sold.
And they wouldn't take 'em.
They not supposed to take 'em.
They leave that the way they are.
But in another way, they always take a little.
They always try to beat the Indians
  because the king is not really satisfied.
Coyote told 'em,

> "You can put that down.
> And you going to make a book right in the same town.
> Then when you get them finished,
>   it's a book.
> You gonna give 'em to my children.
> By this time, my children, they can read.
> Then you give 'em this book.
> That's *their* law.

When they get that, then they can read it.
And then they know that's their law."

But the king, he didn't make that stuff.
They didn't make it.
They do some, just a little and they leave it alone.
And they never do anything until he die.
And another king, that was his son.
See the paper.
They work on that and leave 'em.
They don't finish 'em.
For a long time, and he die.
And another one.
Still the same.
The third king, they never.
The old one, that's the four.
They told 'em, they don't want to finish it. They don't want to do it.
So, because king, the first king, he was not satisfied,
  he was forced by Coyote,
    and this other king, he still had that idea.
So in another way, God knows that.
They want to change.
They don't want to have a king—a man.
They want to have a queen.
Got to be a woman.
So, this last time, the king, they got no boy.
They got no boy but they got two daughters.
When he die, they always be a boy of the king.
When the king die, then the boy willl be king.
Or if no boy, maybe not.
Maybe close relative, then they can be king.
But this time, no boy, no relatives close to him.
They got two daughters.
And the people over there in England,
  they decided, and they thought about it.
There is no way.
They got no son that is going to be the king.
Finally the one of them was saying,

    "What about the womans?

They got two daughters.
The older one, they going to be the queen."

"No."

At that time, you know,
  because the woman is not allowed to be in the business like that.
But for a long time, and some of them said,

"Well, that should be all right.
That was his daughter.
If we had her for a queen, it'll be just as good."

But the others, no.
So they just go about, just about half-and-half.
They can't get nowhere.
The other ones, they say,

"All right, we'll put up for a queen."

And the other ones say no, no, no.

Again, God's thought.
They figure out these people,
  they going to make some kind of a machine.
They make a kind of bird, you know, the little bird,
  just like kids were playing now.
They might make little bird
  and they can run around or fly.
They say they can make one of them.
And they put ...
And they could tighten spring, tighten.
And big room.
Lotta people in there.
And they could let 'em go.
Let that bird fly around in the room.
When they come to someone head,
  sit right on top there.
It's gotta be three times for the same one.
And that'll be the queen or king.
Any of them.

All right. They make that.
When they get them finished, they call the people in the big room.
Full of people.
Man and womens all mixed.
So they tighten that and let them go.
Fly around.
They come on the head of that queen, the daughter, the older one,
  right on her head.
They not satisfied.
They tighten 'em again and let 'em go.
Fly around the same way.
Three times.
That's all.
She's the queen.
Then, when she become to be queen,
  and look at the paper and find out for long time,
    they find out that her grandfather, great grandfather,
      and grandfather, all along,
        they never do this, never do the work.
They suppose to do it but they never did.
So she thought to herself,

> "When I am queen, I am going to do it.
> It's not good.
> My grandfather, great grandfather,
>   my grandfather and all them ... "

So she decides to do it,
  because it's supposed to be done.
So she finish 'em—a book, good and thick.
Thicker than this and bigger.
They make four of them,
Four books, all the same but four.
That's quite a while ago.
Could be over a hundred years or more since they finish that book.
Then, they had 'em all finish.
That's the Indian law.
That's where the Indians' law—in that book.
Nothing but Indian law.
And that's what they call "The Black and White."

Because whoever made that law, one of 'em was black
  and the other one was white.
See, that's the king, that was white.
And Coyote was black—was an Indian.
"Black and White."
They made that law.
That's the reason why they call that book, "Black and White,"
  the law, they call the law, "Black and White."
Then, they have this book four of them.
That's about, could be somewhere around 1850.
Somewhere around that time.
I couldn't be sure.
I like to find that out some of these days.
And he sent this book, they sent a man right from England.
And they give 'em this book—the four of them, the three of them.
And the queen kept one right in the office there.
But they give the three to this man.
And they tell this man,
  after the book was finish and they write a separate letter,
    just like a while ago, write a separate letter.
And he did that.
And he put that separate letter in the book like that.
And they write that and they said to this man,

> "When you get to Ottawa,
>   you go in the Parliament and you tell 'em
>   this book is going to be there."

And you tell 'em there was a separate letter in there,
  to take that out and read it.
And that writin' says,

> "You keep that book for a long time
>   'til the Indians get to be educated so they can read,
>   so they can be good enough to understand
>   that book by reading
>   For quite a while, then you just take it
>   and just hand it to the Indian.
>   And let them open it and read it.
>   Then they can see that's theirs.
>   That's the first book, you leave it in Ottawa.

79

Then you take the others ones,
   in halfway in Canada—that would be in Winnipeg,
    that's the halfway.
Between Ottawa and Victoria.
And you put the other book in the Government House,
   just like in the Parliament.
Same way. They write and put 'em in there.
And tell 'em to get that right away and read.
When they read that, they suppose to keep that book
   for so long
     'til the Indians would be understand, go to school,
      and get to understand,
        they can get good education so they can read that book
        to understand."

Then they take the other one to Victoria.
When they come to Kelowna, that man,
  and they want the Indian to take 'em
   from Kelowna to Hope on the horseback.
No plane, no automobile, no wagon road, no buggy
  because no wagon road.
Only pack horse, saddle horse.
That's around 1850 or 1860.
Because in 1863 when they built this trail here.
Just a trail.
They were like that everywhere at that time.
But this man, I don't know how he get to Kelowna.
But he come to Kelowna.
But that time Kelowna just a little town, something like Keremeos.
But he wanted the Indian, for the Indian to use his horses.
Indian can be guide [to] him, take him to Hope.
Then from Hope, they can take the boat from Hope to Westminster.
Whether the Parliament was still at Westminster at that time,
  or it had moved to Victoria, the capital.
That's something I didn't know for sure.
But is taking to the government, now they call it the BC Government.
So they get a man from Westbank, an Indian guy.
And this guy, his name must be TOH-mah.
But the Indians, they call him, Toh-MAT, but they don't say it right,
  you know.
His name was TOH-mah.

That's all the name I know.
I don't know his second name.
Or, his first name,
Maybe his first name, maybe TOH-mah,
  maybe that was his second name.
Or maybe that was his first name, I don't know.
Only name I know, that was TOH-mah.

When I seen him in 1917, and I was seventeen at that time.
When I seen him, he was kinda way older than me now.
See, I am eighty years old now.
But the time when I seen 'em in 1917, he's more than eighty.
Pretty old.
I seen him in Penticton.
I seen him twice.
Then he's the one, he bring that man.
He take his pack horse and another horse for him to ride,
  and himself ride.
And he leadin' the pack horse.
And they come from Westbank all along there
  and then they come to Keremeos.
And they went on this road, bridge and they went over the trail
  from Princeton.
Then when they get there, in the halfways
  from Princeton on the summit,
    that's on the trail, not on this road now.
That's different way.
So over the mountain and there was a summit.
When they get to the summit, noon time,
  then it was in the summer, like in September, they say getting' to be fall
    when they took that man over.
When they come to the summit, just about noon,
  then this white man told TOH-ma,

        "We stop here and make a lunch."

Because when they do, TOH-ma, they always do the cookin'.
And do the packing.
He do everything.

And that man, they don't anything, you know,
  they can't do any work.

So they stop and undo the pack horse, they build a fire,
  and do the cookin' and eat.
After dinner, white man, they pick up a blanket like that nice blanket.
And they go out on nice grass, nice ground and put the blanket there.
And they lay down and take the suitcase and open 'em
  and pull out a lot of paper and lay them there
    and then he read 'em.

And TOH-ma he jump around, wash the dishes
  and fix up everything ready to go.
And this man told him,

> "Should not pack 'em.
>   We not go.
>   We stay here for the rest of the day.
>   And we stay here overnight.
>   We give the horses a chance to rest.
>   And we rest.
>   We gonna stay here this afternoon."

All right.
TOH-ma, he speak in Chinook, the both of 'em.
So when TOH-ma finish everything and then the white man told him,

> "You can put up a tent.
>   We can sleep in there.
>   You never know, maybe tonight it might rain."

So he went and put up tent.
Finish and he put up everything.
And that could be around two o'clock or something like that.
And this white man told TOH-ma,

> "Did you finish?

> "Oh yeah, I finish everything."

All right, he tell him,

> "You come here."

So TOH-ma, he went.

The white man told him,

> "I want you to see this book."

TOH-ma says,

> "I can see 'em all right.
> But I don't know what's in there.
> I can't read 'em."

Well, told him,

> "Well, I didn't want you to read that.
> I know you can't read.
> But there was some picture in that book that I want to
>   show you,
>   that picture, see if you know.
> If you don't know, you tell me,
> But if you know, you tell me."

So, this TOH-ma, they kinda lay down
  and the white man put that book there.
Showed it to him.
Says,

> "Did you see that picture?"

TOH-ma, he looked at that picture,
  he can tell right away that's Coyote.
And white man asked him,

> "You know this picture?"

TOH-ma says,

> "Yeah, I know who's that.
> That's Coyote. That's Coyote.
> That's the king for the Indians.
> Coyote.
> But he's not here.
> He's down, way down in the South Seas.
> Right in the water."

White man says to him,

"Right. You know all right."

Then he shows him another picture of Coyote.
Quite a few picture because when they were in England,
  and the king, they take picture of him, you know,
    quite a few.
So, this white man told TOH-ma,

"This is the last book.
  Now I'm getting to Hope.
  Now I went on the boat from Hope and get to the Capital
    then I'm going to leave that book in there.
  That's the Indian book.
  But it's going to be there for some times.
  They can give to the Indians,
    a long time from now
      when the Indian can get to be educated and read.
  So that would be the time they suppose to get 'em.
  And there was two of 'em.
  I left one in Ottawa.
  And I left one in halfways.
  And this is the last one.
  There's three of them I brought from England.
  The queen give me these books.
  They sent me.
  Now I am going over there.
  We can go as far as Hope
    and you can come back but I go on the boat."

So that's the way the Indian knows about it, these books that was there.
And now today still there in Victoria.
And the other one in Winnipeg.
And the other one in Ottawa.

And I seen that book in Victoria in the capital.
And we think that was the one.
They was big, about this long and about this wide.
This is black.
And it was locked.
Padlocked.

Little padlock, about that size.
Right on the table.
I and Tommy Gregoire and Andrew Paul.
We seen that.
And Andrew Paul is the one that talk.
So we think, I and Tommy,
  he should open this paper to show what he see.
But he never said nothing. He never move.
They lay there.
They never touch 'em or nothing.
So that's the one all right.
That's the "Black and White."
We seen 'em.

And since that time it was told,
  to give to the Indian when the Indian they can read.
That would be now today because all these Indians everywhere,
  they can read.
Just like white people.
It's only me because I didn't have enough school.
So they should give 'em by now.
But before this time, then they figure, hide that.
They should not give 'em to the Indian.
They hiding 'em.
But they never throw 'em away.
They never burn 'em.
They still keep 'em but they wouldn't show them to the Indian
  unless the Indian say about and ask 'em about.
That's the way it was nowadays.

And a lot of these Indians they don't know about that.
And they talking about land claim, "Land Question."
But they go to mention about it,
  how come for them to say this claim in my land.
They got to say the right word.
If they don't, well, they were beat.
And a few years ago, about '43.
1943.
And I see that in 1947.

THEY TELL 'EM ALL ABOUT WHAT THE WHITE PEOPLE HIDING FROM THE INDIANS

*Stories about whites and their ways were much sought
after. But getting access to these stories was difficult.*

My grandmother, her mother was a half-brother [means half-sister]
  to John P. Curr.
My grandmother was uncle [means niece] to him.
And it seems to ...
  well, they don't live together, but they right there, you know.
That's their neighbour.
And every time they tell these stories
  and my grandmother was kinda old enough then to listen.
And they do.
They listen.
They want him.
They say,

   "That's a good idea. Stay when I tell the stories."

And that is why my grandmother knows a lot of stories from him.

And when I become to be six years old
And they begin to tell me,
  they keep on tellin' me every once in a while seems to be,
    right along 'til 1918.
And she died when she was 85.
So that's how it is for me to know a lot of things, a lot of stories—
  what is going to go, and what is been going and so on.

And not only that.
But I heard something like that from these others, like Pierre John's dad.
He was a chief.
And he's got a brother-in-law, a white man named Jameson.
Good man too.

He come from Kentucky.
And he got here in British Columbia.
And he wanted a girl to marry.
And that John Shiweelkin's daughter—sister to, brother to—
  Pierre John's father.
And Jameson, he marry her.
And he become to ...
He's brother-in-law to John Ashnola, John Shiweelkin—
  Pierre John's dad.
That's his brother-in-law.
And this Jameson, he's a good man.
He's good educated and so on.
He knows a lot of things.
And he come and tell the old man to tell some stories
  and tell some certain things.

And they keep doing that.
He tell his brother-in-law some kind of things—
  how it's going to be later on from that time 'til later and for now.
And that's how that John knows.
And my wife was his daughter.
And he tells the stories to his children.
Most the time.
My wife, they learn all that.
She's got a good head.
And she's the one that tell me, her dad,
  the things he know from his brother-in-law, Jameson.
But Pierre John, he don't care much.
And there's a lot of this, he don't know.
He don't care.
And he's too young anyway.
That's another one I learn.

And my grandfather, he works to one white man down ...
  they call 'em now Palmer Lake, in this end of Palmer Lake.
The farmer's name was Palmer.
He put in, made a ranch there.
And my grandfather works for him.
Building a fence, cutting rails, building a fence, no wire fence those days.
They cut a poplar, split them, some other rails.
They make rails for a fence.

Snake fence ...
No barb wire.
They don't send it this far.
They might have some back east, but they don't come here.
And they do that work for that ranch.
They lived there.

And this Palmer, they seems to like him.
Must be a good worker.
They works there a long time.
And Mr. Palmer, they thought maybe they tell him a lot of things.
Had a good idea to let him know.
So he did.
And what the stories that they tell him,
  it's something like the stories that my grandmother hear from her uncle.
It's almost the same, you know.
It's likely the same the stories, but likely different in one way or another.
So that way I learned some more from my grandfather.

And my uncle, my mother's brother.
He's got a brother-in-law.
And his brother-in-law goes with the priest.
He carries the priest around on the pack horse.
Always travels on the pack horse those days.
And he helped him to pack.
And he helped him to put in a camp.
And he do the cooking for him.
And he take care of him, the priest.
And the priest is kind of middle age.
But himself is younger.
Good worker.
And he good friends with the priest.

And finally the priest, they begin to tell him a lot of things.
And he tell to my uncle, to his brother-in-law,
So my uncle tell me that.

So that's another way I learned the story.
Not only from one.
I learned from quite a bunch.

And they call 'em, Mary Narcisse.
She's the one that lived up 'til 116.
She tell a lot of stories.
And she tell me a lot of things.
There's quite a few different things I learned, the stories.
A lot of things.
That's why I know.

Wendy: Not too many other people tell stories like you do.

No, because nobody tell 'em.
They don't know.
But I was told enough.
I was told.
I got enough people to tell me.
That's why I know.

Wendy: And you must have a good memory.

Well, it could be I guess.
I forget.
I don't care for it and I forget.
But the older I get, seems to come back on me.
Supposin' if the radio, you could see the picture goin' by.
Something like that, I could see, like, and remember.
Older I get.
Maybe God's thought that I should get back and remember so I can tell.
Could be.
I don't know.
But anyway, I was that way.
I like to tell the stories to anybody.
Used to be I thought I could tell only to Indian.
But later on, I thought white people and Indian, they all the same.
I can tell any of them the same stories.
Don't matter.
So now I do that.
I like to tell anyone, white people or Indian.

But a lot of these Indian, they don't believe me.
They don't take my word.

They heard me say something,

> "He don't know. He tell a lie."

But I try to let them know something.
But they wouldn't take my word.

But that's not my fault.

の

Wendy: Your grandmother was in Brewster? And your grandfather went down there?[*]

Yeah, that's right.
She was born, my grandmother, she was born in Brewster.
Her mother there.
But her father is from Ashnola.
Went down there and married down there.
Then she was born there.
And that's Skeuce's son.
But Shiweelkin was a brother, full brother to Skeuce.
And that was his son, the one that went down to Brewster
  to marry a girl down there.
And my grandmother born.
And her father is from Standard Rock.

And she come back with my grandfather,
You know, my grandfather.
But he's part Thompson, my grandfather.
But they really born around in this area.
And he grow up, but got some people in Thompson.
So that is why my grandmother is, her father is from here.
But they got married and come back here.
That's the way it goes.

Wendy: So what was your grandmother's name?

My grandmother, Louise.
Louise, that was her name.
Married to Joseph Newhmkn.

---

[*] This section was part of another conversation. I have included it here because it fits with the subject matter of the preceding section.

And see?
Her name Louise Newhmkn.
So I took that name for my Indian name, Newhmkn.

Wendy: And what does that mean?

That means roan back of horse.
Horse, roan back.
Not roan altogether, but just the back.
Roan back.
Maybe just where the saddle is.
That's kind of a roan.
But the rest of the hair, may black or may white or something.
Not roan altogether.
Just roan in the back. That's what it means.

Wendy: And what was your mother's name?

My mother, Arcell.
Arcell, you write that down yesterday.
She never was married.
All her life.
She never was married.
She died when she was eighty-three in 1958.

So that ...

Wendy: Did she tell stories too? Your mother?

Oh no.
She never.
She never.
She tried to tell me something, but just a little.
She never tried to tell me.

Wendy: Just your grandmother?

Just my grandmother.
Because they live together.
That's why my mother never was married
Because they can't leave.
They don't want to leave the old folks.
They always a daughter.
But these old folks, they got three sons.

The one of 'em died.
By frozen.
Mail carrier, and they froze on the way carrying the mail.
Round Oliver in the end of Osoyoos Lake.
But the other two, one of them is married up in Westbank way.
And the other one was married down in Kartar, they call 'em.
Between Omak and Nespelem.
That's one of 'em married.
Their son.
And they go over there this one here they live here all the time.
But this other one, he lives there once in a while away from his
	father-in-law.
They got a lot of property, a lot of cattle, a lot of horses and things.
Big ranch.
And my uncle they good worker.
Work for his father-in-law for sometimes, but come back.
And round here, they get job.
They handy.
They kinda carpenter and things like that.
And they build a log house from some people.
And they get paid.
My uncle, that's the other one—
	that's Joe, his name.
Take the name of his dad, Joe Newhmkn.
His dad was Joe too, Joseph Newhmkn.

Well, he's Joseph too.
But the other one, up there, Paul, his name.
Paul Newhmkn.

And my mother, she got a sister younger than her.
But she died when she was about twelve, thirteen years old.
And she died.

And she's the only daughter for these old folks.
And she don't like to leave.
Because if she do, well, these old folks, they can't get along.
Too old.
They got to be there to take care of the old people.
And that's why they never was married to my dad.

Because if they do, my dad gonna bring her to his people.
But she don't like it. She likes to stay at the old folks'.

And they tell my dad,

> "If you come, if you stay with my old folks right here,
>   we will marry."

But my dad,

> "There's nothing there for me to stay.
>   I wouldn't stay there. I'd sooner stay at my folks'."

All right, they separated.
And my dad too.
He lives there with his folks.
And my mother lives there with her folks.
And that's where I grow up.

And as soon as I can remember when I was five.
See? I remember when I was three years old.

   Wendy: You told me that.

But I come to remember better when I get to five or six.
Then my grandmother—
   see, my mother goes out work, maybe goes out work for somebody.
For garden, for things like that.
Or maybe washing clothes.

They always go work.
Or else they grow up their own garden.
And they goes and work their own garden
   while I and grandmother stay home.
My grandmother is blind.
She can see but not far.
And somebody's got to be with 'em all the time.
If they wanted something, they got to send somebody.
That would be me.

And that's why I stay with her at all times.
And when we together just by ourselves

And she tell me,

> "Come here."

And I sit there while she hold me.
And she tell me the stories kinda slow.
She want me to understand good.

For all that time until I got to be bigger, sixteen.
Still tell me stories 'til she die in 1918 when she was eighty-five.
And she don't tell me stories no more.

Wendy: You and your grandmother must have been pretty close?

Oh yeah, we sit together most the time when she was alive.

So, that was the stories about John P. Curr.
They figure they could learn the Indian—
   he's half-Indian.
His dad, you know, full white man.
But John P. Curr is half-white and half-Indian.
And his dad want him to tell his Indian side,
   what he have learn from his white side.
That's the idea.
And he did.
Because it's got to be person like him, half-and-half.
Half right in both sides.

So those days.

But since, a lot of things changed.
See, at one time that I remember, the half-breed,
   they just leave 'em alone.
Send him to school.
Or some of 'em didn't.
Those days it's different.
'Til they get old enough to know everything.
Get to be twenty or twenty-one.
Then it's really up to him if it was a boy.
Really up to him to say,

> "I'm going to be on my Indian side. I can be Indian."

All right, they could say that at the law.
Once they said that, it was written down.
It's got to be that way the rest of his time.
Indian.
But if he says,

> "Well, I can be on my white man's side.
> I can be 'white man.'"

All right, that's written down.
Got to be that way all his time.

But if he's on Indian,
  they can be Indian as long as he want
    'til he make up his mind to change to white.
They can do it.
They can change to be white member.
But never go back to the reserve no more.
But in another way, don't have to.

So that is the law for the half-breed.
It's really up to him to say which side it can be.
Can't be on both ways.
Can be on one of them.
But the other one, they might have the blood in them—
  white but mostly Indian.
Well, that's Indian.

That's the law that I know at one time.
Supposed to be still that way.
But a lot of people they don't want that.
That's not good.
Maybe it's law but not right.
And they make a new one.
What they make the law, whoever they make, some of the Parliament,
But God didn't make that law.
Unless God says so, whatever he says should be the law
Supposed to be followed, that was a law.
But if someone around here, I can make the law myself.
And then, not God. I did that myself.
It's not a law.

That's what they do—a lot of people.
Might be a government member.
But he decided, him and another one, two or three of them.
They make a new law.
They think they do it.
They do it all right.
But God didn't say so.
Not okay that.
It's not a law.
But a lot of people take that.
Because *Stin*, he's a really good talker.
See, that's another help the other way.
Do you understand about *Stin*?
He's bad.

And Jameson, John's brother-in-law,
He lives up at the Five Mile Creek.
He took that place for his ranch.
And he grow up some ranch in there.
But John he lives over there across the river, just a little way,
   about two miles from here.
And once in a while he come.
There is no trail on the other side of the river.
But he go across the river, him and his wife.

And they go along that way where there is no trail, nobody around.
And they go all along to get to John's place.
When they get there, they seems to hide.
If somebody, some Indian or some white man come,
   they go in the other room or go upstairs
      so nobody know that he was there.
But when the night comes, and they put curtains on the window,
   black blankets or something like that so nobody could see from outside.
And they be sittin' all night, him and his brother-in-law and his wife.
Because they tell a lot of things to his brother-in-law.
If he can't understand in some, even if it was Chinook,
   but his sister can do the interpreting between the two of them.
That's why he take his wife along to go to see John to tell him stories.
And what she have tell him,
And he says to John,

"These, what I tell you now, it will never come soon.
Not right away.
You don't need, well I tell you to know,
   but maybe you wouldn't use it,
      maybe you still afraid.
But just in case you should know.
Supposin' if you got stuck in some way,
   you can use some of these words that I tell you.
And the government man, he will ask you,
   'Where did you learn that? Who told you that?'
That's what the question he will ask you.
And you can tell 'em,
   'Well, the Indians, they know things from way back.
      And that has been carried.'
Don't tell 'em that I tell you.
If you tell 'em 'Jameson tell me,'
   they go over there to policeman
      and they take me up and put me in jail.
Put me to trial.
And I get a sentence to be in jail the rest of my time.
Or else, they could put rope on me and raise me up.
That's the way they going to do with me
   if they know I am going to tell you that.
Because I am white man and I am not supposed to tell you.
But in another way I got to tell you.
So don't say.
But whenever I die, and I'll be buried,
   then you use these words that I been telling you.
And they will ask you,
   'How do you know? Who tell you?'
You could say, 'Jameson tell me.'
And what could they do to me?
I am already buried!"

See?
That might be quite important, what they have tell him.
Could be because they try to hide them.
And they tell 'em all about
  what the white people hiding from the Indians.
And I know that.

I learn that from the other people,
  from my grandmother, John P. Curr stories.
But still I learned from them too.

See?
They, the white people, they think they clean everything,
  land and Indian people and everything.
And they can have them.
They got the power because they got the paper.
God let them have the paper so far so they could use it for themselves.
But the Indians, they give 'em a law in their brains.
They remember.
See?
That's why I always say the white people and the Indians,
  they not the same way.
The Indians, they got a different way.
And the white people they got different way.
But sometimes they get together
And there'll be all in one line.
But not all the time.
Sometimes they go apart for a while and get together again.
But the white people they want 'em to be together all time.
But God didn't say that.
God says can be that way whatever he said,
  to set that law
    and he says can be that way until the end of the world.
Who knows when the world is going to end?
But he says this is going to be that way 'til the end of the world.

So Coyote is supposed to send back before the world end.
He's got to send.
And he's in the sea now today, Coyote.
I seen the picture of that.
Just like the one I seen you give me.
Something like that but they were sittin' in the boat.
Sittin' in the boat.
Half of the boat, big boat.
Big, wide.
Half of the boat was kind of a shack.
They got a roof on 'em.
And they got a door.

And they go in there and sleep there.
But on the outside, see the shack was just about half of the boat.
But the other half is a boat like that;
  and they got a fire there, open fire.
Day and night.
Never go out.
That's where they cook.
And that's where they sittin' to get warm.
But if it rain, goes in there, in the shack.
Got a bed in there.
Right in the sea.
Can never get to the shore.
God don't allow him to get to the shore.
They want 'em to be in the sea way out.

And it was.
The Indians, they know that.
They talked about it.
They know Coyote, they in the sea.
God put him to be there for the lifetime.
Well, that means he got a sentence from God to have a life sentence.
Be there 'til almost the end of the world.
And he can talk and he can go around like he used to be ...
Maybe he can travel on a plane or something.
So the Indians know it was that way.

THAT ONE YOU FELLAS KILLED, HE COME ALIVE!

A Similkameen chief finds himself in
the wrong place at the wrong time.

This man, he's a full white man.
His name, John P. Curr.
I had 'em written down but I don't know what I did with it.
And this John P. Curr is a full white man.
And he's a young man only, might be twenty-two.
Maybe twenty-three because they finish school.
They don't go to school no more.
But they can go to school for the job they going to do.
Anybody do that.

So that was the man.
And he can be a government man.
And he was a government man already.
But all he got to do is got to be teach, like.
And later on he got to go in the government office
  wherever they are.
Maybe Portland, Seattle or anywhere in the big city.
And later on they want him to be in the White House.

Okay.
His dad, his father and his grandfather, they all government man.
But his son can be a government man as well as he.
That's the way it goes.
And he's younger, John P. Curr.
John P. Curr was the grandson of the old government man.
And his dad, they got that from way back.
He tell the Indian all that.
Then this time, he go to school for long enough.
And he out of school.
And he started on the job.

But he was a government man.
But different job that he started.
They bring a bunch of man and women.
The man is supposed to be fully man.
And nine women.
They brought that from Portland
  up the river 'til they get to Walla Walla.
And they come on that side.
Come through the big bend.
But they gotta cross someplace on the ferry.
They got some ferry down there already then.
And they could be somewhere around 1830 or 1825,
  something like that.
Because he's only young then.

And they bring this bunch of people.
And all the horses they got—over a hundred.
They pack horses.
And the horses they were riding, they all riding.
From Portland.
They moving to Vancouver.
Then from Vancouver, they might take the boat
  to move to some part of Alaska.
See?
That belongs to, you know, Alaska is the States.
So, those days they can only travel on the sea, on the water.
No trail.
Thick timber on the edge of the lakes in the west.
No roads.
There mighta be trail but big bunch of pack horses,
  they can't drive 'em through there.
And he got nowhere to eat.
They got no grass.
There just timber, thick timber.

So they have to move with the horses from Portland up the river.
Or, they come across from Portland.
See? The river goes that way to Walla Walla.
That turned to Portland.
Then they cross to Portland on the ferry, horses and everything.
And they make a shortcut and they got into Columbia River

on the other side of Brewster at Wenatchee or somewhere in there.
But they cut all that back.
In other way, they have to come over that side and they come on this side
    and across that way.
They stop where the horses can have feed, where they got some grass.

That's the idea.

If they move that way, they can never get through.
No road, no trail, only boat.
But just bunch of horses. Over a hundred head.

So they can't haul 'em, I don't think, those days.
They might have a boat but they can haul only some.

And, a bunch of these horses,
    they want to leave 'em in Chilliwack to be used.
They can take some of that, take 'em to Vancouver and use 'em.
But whenever they don't use 'em, bring 'em back to Chilliwack.
That can be their home for the horses.
This is mostly pack horses and saddle horse.
They need it those days.
No motorcycle, no bicycle, no car, no airplane, no nothing.
Only saddle horse.
That's a long time ago.

So they move there—a bunch of men.

Then, I don't know if they got across from Portland this way
    or else, I think they go up on the first trail.
And then they come along by Walla Walla.
And then they come quite a ways up.
Then they cross the one ferry down in there.
Someplace, I don't know just whereabout.

So this old ferry, it mighta be changed by now.
Mighta be nothing there.
Nobody knows they have a ferry.
I know one of them before but I did tell you.
But they not there.
There are no people there no more.
There's a lot that went that way.

So they get moving, this bunch of pack horses.
They pack a lot of groceries and some implements.
Some plough, maybe some of the implements to work on the farm.
Not like they are now.
Those days they are different
  but that's the only thing they could use on the farm.
They pack those and a lot of groceries.

And all these mans, the forty men,
  they going to stay in Vancouver.
Some of 'em going to stay in Vancouver.
And some of them, they go to Alaska.
So they take 'em as far as Vancouver anyway.
Then they supposed to come back—this young men.
He's the boss.
The others were just working men.
But anyway, altogether there was forty.
But there was a man, fifteen, maybe twenty,
  to pack the horses, you know.
But he's the boss, John.

So they come along and they come by,
  where they call now, they call Brewster.
And those days, that's not the name.
They had a name in Indian.
And the names in Indian is Kor-A-tin.
That one little mountain is just nothing
  but yellow like this sunflower at this time of year.
And you can see that from long ways.
One little round mountain.
And just nothing but sunflowers.
And they could see 'em from long ways.

Look all yellow.
The whole mountain.
Not too high. Just kinda small mountain.
And they give 'em that name, Kor-A-tin.
That name is kind of a yellow mountain
  or yellow hill or something like that.
But this Brewster, it mighta be some of the white men been there first.
That would be the name, I guess.

Anyway, they come by there where the town is now today at Brewster.
But there is no town there at that time.
Only Indians.
Lot of 'em there.
And another bunch this side
  where the Okanogan* and the Columbia River gets together.
And there was another big bunch of Indians right at the join of the
  two rivers.
And the others farther down after Brewster.
Then some more down the river just little bunches
  all along the Wenatchee.
Not very big bunch.
Small group.

But this is the most at Brewster.
And they call that in those days, *N-kum-SHEEN*.
That's in Indians.
That means the two rivers get together.
Join together and then go in one river.
But that's in Indian word there.
And they got a different word for that in Thompson, in Kamloops.
They call it Kamloops, see?

They come by.
They see a lot of Indians where the town is now.
But they don't stop.
They ask some of the Indians and they tell 'em:

> "You go up a little ways yet."

Supposin' if they know the mileage.
Maybe five, six miles yet to go.
Then they could find a way better place for the horses.
Lots of range, lotta grass.

> "That's the place you want to stop
>   because you have a lot of horses."

---

* Note that the spelling of "Okanagan" changes south of the international border. The river that bears this name is the "Okanogan"; and the term for the Aboriginal peoples of the region is "Okanagon."

Then there was some Indians just across the river,
  small river.
They call that Okanogan River.
They comes into Columbia River.
But right at the join where there are bunch of Indian.
There's two bunches right there.

All right, they kept moving 'til they come.
And they could tell by looking at it,
  that's the place that they was told.
And they stop and unload and camp there.
And the Indians, they know they comin'.
Some of these other Indians and some of these other white mans,
  they got some white people along the river at that time.
And they tell the Indians, they're supposed to be some Indians coming
  with a bunch of pack horses.
They can go by at any time.
And they know.
Somebody tell 'em,

        "They are coming but quite a ways yet down below."

They know they're coming.

When they seen 'em across the river, Okanogan River,
  and they thought they were the bunch.
All right.
They camp there that night.
Next day they stay there.
They don't move because they like the place for the horses.
They like to stay there for about a week or so.
And they give the horses a good rest and good feed.
So finally, this white mans, they holler
  because the Okanogan River is not wide, you know.
And they tell the Indians,

        "Would you come and get us on the canoe?"

They can't ford, you know.
They deep.
They can swim the horses but the other side is no good.
Too steep like that.
Just only certain place they ford, but maybe way up or farther down.

But they have to take 'em on the canoe.
Take 'em on that side.
They wanted to visit,
  John P. Curr, to these Indians.

All right.
Some of the Indians went across.
They had bunch of canoe.
Then they bring the white people across.
And they were together.
They couldn't hardly understand one another.
They can use Chinook language.
But not very many can understand.
A few anyway and they use that for interpret.

So they really enjoy the get-together with the Indians.
Then the Indians, they like to see him and also his bunch.
They left some of the bunch at the camp.
But the others go with him.
Maybe next day the other ones will stay and the other go with him.

So they stayed there.
They ask the chief,

        "Is this your land?"

        "Yeah, this is our land.
          But there was another chief over at the next bunch.
          But it don't matter.
          We all the same group.
          Only we lived apart."

So he was wondering if he could live there for a week or ten days.
The Indians said,

        "All right. You can stay there as long as you want."

He says,

        "Give the horses a rest and feed.
          When the time comes, pack 'em and go."

And, there supposed to be another bunch of white people
  coming from east to meet them bunch,

the one that's coming up the river
　　somewhere, I don't know just where.
But they got the point.
They point at the place.
When they come in, they supposed to meet.
Then, they do when these other boys coming.

And while they were there,
　maybe ten days, maybe fifteen days,
　　and every day they always go across the river
　　　and visit to Indian.

And they want to get a wife from the Indians.
And they ask for the chief.
And they ask who is the father of this girl.
And told 'em.
And I guess he must have fall in love with the girl anyway
　in the first place.

And they ask the old people,
　the dad and the mom, he says,

　　　　"I want your daughter.
　　　　I want to take her for my wife.
　　　　And later on we can go and marry.
　　　　But we can't marry here because there is no one to marry
　　　　　people here."

Those days in Brewster there.
But they do in big town, Walla Walla, Portland.
Was priest, you know.
Too many different kinds of priest.

And they ask the Indian what Catholics do they believe,
　what religion do they believe.
And they told 'em,

　　　　"The preacher, he wears the black clothes.
　　　　They is the one.
　　　　And he carries a big cross, you know.
　　　　A big cross.
　　　　And he carries that.
　　　　We believe in that kind of religion."

Well, that's the Catholic.

> "All right," he said, "That was me too.
> I belong to there.
> Belong to that Catholic way."

So, first the people said,

> "No, you only go by.
> We don't know where you're coming from.
> And you go by and you tellin' us you goin' a long way."

They don't know where is Vancouver those days.
But they find out from him it's quite a ways.

So they tell 'em,

> "We don't want to give you our daughter
>   and take her away too far.
> You may come back. May not."

He says,

> "I will come back."

But they couldn't take his word.
They don't know if he was a government man 'til he told them.
He didn't tell them right away, you know.
They just want to get that woman, that girl for a wife in the worst way.

So, finally most of the people, they talk to one another
  and some of them says,

> "Sounds like a good man.
>   So maybe it's all right to take your daughter
>   and he says he's going to come back.
>   And he said if he take this girl for a wife,
>   And he can leave 'em here.
>   Not to take 'em along.
>   'Til he come back, in about couple of months.
>   When he come back to Brewster, say they going to stay there.
>   Later on, maybe a year or so, they can go down to
>   Portland or Walla Walla

then they can be married and then come back.
And stay there."

But still he's a government man.
He's got the paper.
He make a home there.

So the people thought that would be okay.
So they tell 'em,

"All right."

So finally he got the girl.
For a few days.

"And now," he said, "is the day to move.
I supposed to meet another bunch coming from east.
They got to go by Arrow Lake.
And they supposed to meet at certain place."

And he seems to know.
He never been there.
But they give 'em the name.
And they tell 'em,

"There are always be people along anyway.
You can find that out where about."

All right, he said it's time for him to move.
Then he pack up all the horses.
Then he move.

He left his wife at their folks'.

So they come a ways, maybe the next day or two after that.
Then they met this bunch again like he was,
  something like him.
They bring bunch of people.
But that's suppose to be from Canada.
But they go into the States.
And they suppose to go down to Portland.
But they meet them there.
So they could see one another and talk to one another.

And these other ones, they go to the States,
  but him, they go this way, go to Vancouver.
And these others, the ones that come from east,
  they come by at Arrow Lake.
And there was a lot of Indians at Arrow Lake.
And they hire one of these Indians for guider.
Interpreter.
They can speak in Chinook good
  because they had the priest in that area first.
Then the rest of the Indians this way.
So the priest teach 'em how to speak in Chinook.
And a few of them could speak good.
And he's one of them.
So they said,

> "All right.
>   You go with us for now 'til we meet the bunch
>   that's coming from below.
>   When we meet there, that's going to be the bunch
>   that you going to work.
>   But we just getting you from Arrow Lake.
>   Whenever we meet them, you can go with them.
>   But we keep going that way.
>   We hire you for these people.

So they meet these people, that John P. Curr outfit.
And then he says,

> "This is the man you want.
>   That will be your guider
>   all the way to Chilliwack and Vancouver."

All right.
So that's the way that Indian from Arrow Lake,
  he comes with this second pack train
    that comes up the river.
Well, the first anyway, but the second from coming that way.
So he switch there and go to the other bunch.
And then he go along with him.
But he knows quite a bit of this country.
He must have been around before.
He must have know as far as Hope.

Those days they work on the pack train and they get as far as Hope.
All the way, but he doesn't go from Hope
  down to Chilliwack and also straight down to Vancouver.
So he got started to work there.
And he speaks in the Okanagan language.
That's the language they use over there in Arrow Lakes.
Same language as we use here in the Okanagan.

So they seems to be okay to come in here in the Similkameen.
They understand.
That's their language—what they use here.

All right.
They're coming and the others keep going towards Portland.
But these other ones keep coming this way.
But John, he left his wife at the Indians, at the Forks, still there.
But when he come back from Vancouver,
  they not going to go any further.
They going to be there, he says.

All right, they kept a-comin'.
All the way and somebody told 'em, this man from Arrow Lake,
  he know the place, but not very good.
He seems to forget.
Only once to go by there.
And he missed that creek, that Spotted Lake Creek.
This is the creek that should have come up to Spotted Lake.
Then they can get into Richter Pass in that valley.
Then come into Similkameen Valley.
They miss that.
They went too far near the lake that way.
And they couldn't spot the place.
They should be higher and then they would know the place.
But no road those days.
It's all open.
But if it was kind of a narrow valley, they got a trail they can follow.
But in the prairie, they can go anywhere.
No certain mark of trail.
So that's why they miss that place.
And they pass and they kept going 'til they get to Okanagan Falls.
And they get that far before they know.
They went too far.

They supposed to go over to the end but they come this way too far.
And they found some Indians there.
And some of the Indians tell 'em,

>"Keep going and get to Penticton.
>   And there were a lot of Indians there.
>   There was a creek up that way.
>   You might have to follow that creek.
>   There is Indian everywhere and they could tell you which
>   way to go.
>   And then you will get into Similkameen Valley later on.
>   But you have to come back quite a ways, ten to fifteen miles.
>   Something like that."

So they kept moving.
And they get by Penticton—there is no town yet then.
Might be one or two houses or white people lived there those days.
But mostly Indians on this side.
But just a few white people on that side.
That's what they were saying.
And when they left, these Penticton Indians,
  they tell 'em to go up on the bench.

>"When you get up on the bench,
>   that's better for the horses.
>   Then you follow that bench 'til you come to the end of the
>   bench.
>   And you get into the same creek.
>   And then you can go a little ways."

And that's where Armstrong is now.

>"And that's the forks of the two creeks.
>   Then you take the south fork and follow that.
>   And there'll always be an Indian at anywhere to show you
>   where to go."

They follow that.
Only trail those days.
No truck road.

So they come to that place where that road goes now

112

to the skidding [means skiing] place.
And there was some Indians there.

And told 'em not to go that way.
That goes in the wrong direction.
They don't get nowhere in the valley.
They go up on the mountain and they turns to the north.
Then they get lost that way.

> "Follow this canyon this way.
>> And pretty soon you come to a creek.
>> And later on you come to another one.
>> And these two creeks, they get together and they run down
>>> towards Keremeos.
>> Follow this creek.
>> One place, it's not too far.
>> It's kinda bad.
>> You might make a trail to go by there.
>> But as you go by there, then you okay.
>> The rest of the way, there was a trail.
>> You can go through 'til you get there to Keremeos.
>> Then you have to go around the mountain.
>> Then see the valley up.
>> And that's the way you supposed to go to Princeton.
>> Then from Princeton, someone,
>>> they will tell you and also that Kootenay Indian,
>>>> they been through there once or twice.
>> They know the way.
>> Different trail those days.
>> Trail been changed since, twice, I think.
>> And now the wagon road.
>> I been through that trail while it was a trail yet, in 1918.
>> But that's the new trail."

So they went that far.
And they go over the mountain and they stop on the summit
  where they can feed the horses.
And someone told them,

> "When you pass that, your horses
>> will never have anything to eat

113

'til you get to Chilliwack.
No grass. Just nothing but timber.
But you got to tough it.
When you get to Chilliwack, well, then it's all kinds of feed.
But that's quite a ways. About fifty miles.
Maybe more.
Nothing to eat for the horses."

Anyway, they keep moving.

Now I passed the story.
That's the way I always do.

But I go back.

While they go by Penticton and they ask the Indians
  how to get into Similkameen Valley,
    and told 'em,

          "All right."

They tell 'em where to go and it will get into Similkameen.
They know already but if they see some more
  they might ask him where to go.
Just there in the part.
And they do.
When they get to follow that bench
  they come into a creek again.
That's the same creek from Armstrong, towards town—
  Penticton is now.
And that's where they meet three, four, maybe five boys.
And they are bad ones.
They are robbers.
Just robbers.
Bad boys. They find that out, these people that go by,
  but they's got to come on the bench and get on that creek.
And then they supposed to try to find to get into Similkameen Valley.
They find that out.
Then they come along to meet them so they could do some robbing
  and things like that.
But these white people, they don't know that.
They think they're just a bunch of Indians riding around.
But they are bad.

They met them there.
And then they talk to them.
And you know how smart bad people was, even today.
They talk to 'em and they think they all good.
And they go along with 'em.
And make a friend with 'em.

And the first thing they know, they stop the horses, all the kitchen pack.
Lot of 'em.
About eight, maybe fifteen.
All the kitchen.
But the others, that was the blanket and tent and other kind of stuff.
So they move that a little more away.
But the kitchen, they figure they going to leave 'em there.
That would be handy for the cooks
    to do some cooking right close to creek.
So these others, they move away.
And while these others are move away
    and these Indian boys, they pull out a rifle
        and they pull out a revolver those days,
            they got single shot only.
Then they says to the white people,

        "I want this pack horse, this and this and this."

They took six pack horses.
All grocery.
They took them and laid 'em out.
If they don't let 'em take it, they'll shoot—the Indian.
But they let 'em take.
They took the pack horses and go.
And when these others come back and they told 'em about,
    they already gone.
And the white people, they know those days.
They should not bother the Indian.
Doesn't matter what the Indian do to them.
Should not bother.
Let them do it.
Let them go.

So they never went after 'em.
But what the Indians done to them, it's bad.

The other Indians, they know that's bad.
So, they just leave 'em.
So they ask the other Indian and they tell 'em where to go.
And also, they follow that 'til they come to the place
   where they can see the Similkameen Valley.
Then they was told that would be the Similkameen Valley
   from the Indian from Kootenay.
Yeah, they been through there once
   and they know that's the Similkameen Valley.

"We got to follow that up north or west."

Then they do.
They keep moving.
And they kept moving 'til they come to Standard Rock.
There is nothing but bunch of grass and good feed.
Good hayfield.
So they thought that would be good place for them to stop.
They stop and camp there.
And they found a few Indians lived there.
And they ask permission to stay there.
And they say,

"All right. You stop there one night or two night."

They stay there for two nights.

Shut it off.
I better quit talking for a while.

Harry continues the story the following day ...

All these people, they supposed to be soldiers.
They had the same clothes, uniform.
And they movin' along.
When they come to Penticton
   (I did mention that but I made a mistake in one word.
      I can see that now.)
I said they took six pack horses' grub.
That's a mistaken word.

Wendy: Really?

I was going to say they had six pack horses—all food.

116

Kitchen-like.
But they took three of them away.
Not six.
See?
I kinda mix up. I know now.

But no, not taken away.
I was going to say,
  they had six pack horses, all kitchen,
    because there was a bunch of them.

But the three of them, three pack horses,
  they were taken away by Indian.
Robbers.
Bad Indians.

So they left.
And they come as far as Standard Rock.

And there was an Indian lived there.
And they asked this Indian if they could stop
  because no fence there at that time.
They are all open.

Said,

      "All right."

The Indian says,

      "Okay, stop here overnight or two if you wanted."

So they stay there for only one night or maybe two.
I don't remember.

And anyway, they move from there.
Not too far.
They move from there this way.
And at Ashnola.
Now today we call it Closed Bridge.
The bridge was there but nobody use them at Ashnola.

They come to that place but there was no bridge then.
That's a long time, you know.

And there was a ford.
They forded the river there.
And that time, and now they straight.
You see the bridge, you go through there.
Cement alongside there.
The lower side, all along.
And it was a trail, but it's kind of a bad place
  for a big bunch of horses.
A few horses, maybe ten head, all right they go by there.
But six or seven pack horses, too many.
They not going to take 'em through that bad place.

So they have to ford there and come on that side.
And then they ford again at Ashnola River.
See? They ford at Ashnola joins to the Similkameen River.
And they come by there.

There was Ashnola River and there were another,
  but that was the same river,
    but it turn out a different direction.
And altogether on this side.

And there were a bunch of Indians had a camp there.
A lot of teepees.
They stay there could be somewhere 'round August
  that is if it was like now.

But they don't know those days.
They always say, "at the chokecherry time."

So now we know that was in August, "chokecherry time."
The chokecherry get ripe and they call that "chokecherry time."
They camp in certain place so they can get the chokecherries.
Eat them and dry 'em.
And that's where the Indians were lived there.
But the same time, they go up hunting up on the mountain.
Get a deer and bring 'em and dry 'em.

And ladies they always go out and pick cherries and dry 'em.
That can be food for the winter.
And these bunch of people came through there.
And five or six man from that Indian camp, they went out hunting.

And the day before the white man came,
  and they already up on the mountain.
And they going to be up there for two, three nights.

And the chief, they have a chief.
And this chief they went with the hunters.
They went along.
He's only about sixty-five that time.
He still goes out with the hunter.

And while they were up on the mountain,
  this bunch of six of them,
    and these people come through there, these white people.
And one of them in the bunch, that's an Arrow Lake Indian,
That is the one that they took from Arrow Lake and they get him down
  somewhere around Brewster or other side somewhere.
And they meet this bunch coming up the river.
So they switch that man to that bunch.
They know they going to make this.
And they suppose to work for that other bunch,
  the one that goes that way.
And he speaks in this language.
He got the same language, the Kootenay Indian as it is here.
Same language.
But this Indian, the one that brought him there,
  he speaks in Chinook too.
Good.

And they have him for a guide.
They take him on the pack train to Hope
  as far as they went.
And come back to Kootenay.

And they hired him to go with this bunch as far as Hope.
That's as far as he knows the country
  but the rest from there, not too far from there to Chilliwack.
They don't know but they can easily find it.

So they could leave the horses right at Chilliwack.
A lot of feed.
And then they could take the boat
  from Chilliwack into New Westminster

and also to Vancouver.
These bunch of people.
Then they could stop in Vancouver for sometimes.
And some of them, they have to go to Alaska.
That's American people.

When they come by Ashnola,
  and they stop.
And these Indians they talk to these other Indians,
  the Indians camped there.
And they ask if they can stop for camping for three, four days
  maybe one week.
If there's any better place up this way.
And they told 'em,

> "Yeah, there one place.
>   Good. That's up here where the church is."

There is no fence.
All that field is now alfalfa.
But those days, they kinda grey more like hayfield.
But there is no grass or alfalfa or anything like that.
Just wild grass. But a lot of feed.

And a big place for a bunch of horses.
They tell 'em, these Indians at Ashnola,
  they tell 'em they could camp there for four, five days
    or one week,

> "It would be good for your horses to have a good rest.
>   And from there, there's not much.
>   Except Princeton, you could stay there awhile too."

All right.
And they come by.
And that chief, Indian chief who went with the hunters,
  and he got six horses in the valley.

He got three mares, every one had a yearling colt.
That makes six.
Maybe they got some new colts too.
But he didn't know where they are.
They turn 'em loose there.

But these horses of his, they go from there
  where that Henry Dennis lives now
    as you come by there.
Some white people lives on both sides of the road.

Then you come by in that van
  another house.
That's where.

And kinda barn. Kinda barnyard in towards the river.
That's Henry Dennis. That's Indian.

And these horses they move from there into that place.
But it's on this side of the river.
But this pack train, it come through on this side.
On that side.
And they ford at Ashnola where the Closed Bridge is now.

And when these hunters came down,
  and they told them about a bunch of white men go by.
And they suppose to stop in this place.

So, the next morning, the chief went down to look for his horses.
He thought maybe his horses goes on with the pack train.
This pack train is not led. They drivin' 'em.
They might go behind, or along, you know.
And they wouldn't know.
Or else, if they did know, they can't get 'em off.
They might be with them right into here.
He think.
But it wasn't.
His horses right over there.
He didn't know.
But he looked around in Ashnola, all that flat.

So he come on that side on horseback to look for his horses.
On that side.
But this pack train, they come across the river,
  where that little town is now.
No nothing there then.
That's only flat. Nothing there.
This pack train they come across the river in that place.

Then they come on this side.
But he kept a-going that way.

So he thought if his horses going along
  they might go on that side.
If not, they might come behind altogether.
But he'll find 'em up here.
He thought.

He was a chief.
And he got a letter from Ottawa.
He know that.
Somebody look at the letter, some white man,
  and tell 'em, "This is your letter from Ottawa from the Parliament."

But, they got to know what that means.
You know, what they tell 'em or something.
So they take that along
  because they know there was an Indian with these white people
    that they could speak in his language and could speak in Chinook.
And he can get white man to read that for him.
And this other man, he could interpret.
And then they'll understand that letter.
That's a good idea.
They bring that along.
And he's going to go to that camp anyway
  where these white men camp.
That's up here at the church.
Up to the hillside there is spring water there at that time.
But since, they bring the water from up on the mountain
  and they run it that way.
Now it's a creek.

But that time, only spring water itself there.

So he came along, came on that side
  and just about there,
    then he go across the river.
And the horses, belong to these white people,
  they put in the camp there.
All in that field.
And this man, he went in there,

and he walk his horse through the bunch of horses
   and look at all the horses.
His horses not there!

All right, well he know his horses, they never come.
They not there.
But they got to go to the camp to show this letter.
He thought.
So they kinda figure maybe they good friends with the white people.
They wasn't there, but this other one tell 'em,

   "You can help there for a few days, don't matter."

So at that time they think,

   "This is only one part, you know."

And, anyway, they went to the camp in afternoon
   about two, three o'clock, something like that.
But the cook, whoever does the cooking for the camp,
   they up to spring water, where they can get water right there,
      and build the fire and do the cooking there.

But the camp, it's farther down, a couple of hundred yards or so.
And that's where the others were there, in the camp.
So they come to that first bench.
But the Indian, the one that's come along from Kootenay,
   he was at the cook's.
He is kinda helper there for the cooks in another way.
In another way he was the guider of the trip.
And in another way he interpret.
See? He got three jobs in that camp.

He didn't know he was up there.
He thought he might be in this camp.
And he ask for him.
But they can't understand to one another.
And these white people, the first bunch they come to,
   they think he is the one that took these pack horses
      from when they come by there.
They think that's one of them.
Maybe the others mighta be hiding someplace.
There's only one show up and look at the horses.

They think they look at *their* horses.
So they thought maybe he size up their horses.
Maybe nighttime or anytime, they might steal the horses.
Take 'em anyway.
That's what they thought.
They didn't know this one, they come from Ashnola here.
So, that's their idea.

But the other one, the other bunch where the cook was,
  that's where the Kootenay Indian.
They didn't know that.

So they took this man, that chief from here.
They took him and they bring him from the camp
  as far as where Squakin house is now.
And no railroad yet that time.
No wagon road.
Only trail.
And took him up to the bench.
Just a small little bench above from the house is now.

And he get him up there.
And they blind him with a handkerchief.
They tie so he can't see.
And they make him sit on the rock.
Boulder, small.
And they make him sit there.
And they blind him.

And they put the gun in the head like that.
They fire.
They pull trigger.
And this man, they fall off and die.

And the bullet, steel bullet ...
That's what they used in those days,
  anytime at wartime.
The bullet they use to shoot one another is a steel bullet.
They don't make no damage when they go through.
They can go through the head.
And just one hole go right through.
No making no damage.

Even in the body if somebody gets shot
  it just go right through.
That's the kind of bullet they give 'em in the head.

Anyway, they died.
And, they never know they had that paper in his shirt pocket,
  that paper he got from Ottawa.
They never look.
They never search.
They just kill him and leave him there.

Leave him right there where they die.
And that was the chief from Ashnola.
His name, Tom.
Tommy Shiweelkin.
They already baptized.
The people around already baptized.
And he took that name, Tommy.
But his father's name, Shiweelkin.
That means "drop of horn."
So his name Tommy Shiweelkin.

And they go back, the soldiers,
  three, four of them.
Bring him and kill him and go back.
  before that Indian knows about that.

But now somebody tell 'em, one of them.

So he said,

          "That's wrong.
            That must be the chief from here.
          Not that one."

So they want to see him.
But he's dead already.
And he said to the others,

          "I'm going over there to take a look."

And they said,

          "Don't go."

So they wouldn't go.
They wouldn't let him go.

But night come.
Towards morning, everybody's sleeping.

So he got up.
And he sneaked out.
They think nobody know.
But some wake up.
And some of them, they knew he went out.
And they tell the others.
And they went after him.

But he come there first.
And he come to that bench.
Getting to be daylight.
He could see better.
And he could see that man was sitting on that rock again.

Come alive, sitting there.
And sitting there and sing his song.
And he took that paper, that letter that he get from Ottawa.
He took that.
It must have been in envelope, but anyway he took that.
He bend 'em like that to keep 'em in the pocket.
And he took that.
And he wiped the blood out from his …
See? He's sitting here.
Wipe that and stamped the paper with his blood.

And he put the paper on the ground
  and he put some stone on it.
So anybody could see that.

But these man who come out and see him,
  they don't go there.
They heard him sing the song and they sitting.
They thought,

> "Well, that's all right. Let him stay that way.
>   He come alive."

So they go down and went back.

But down in the foothill
  and they met the peoples, the one that shot this man,
  the same bunch.

And they come.
And they ask these men,

>   "What you doing here?"

He says,

>   "I go up to see that one you fellas killed.
>   He's alive. He come alive.
>   He's sitting on the rock."

And they couldn't believe it.

They said,

>   "Yeah, they are alive."

So anyways, they say,

>   "All right, well if they are alive,
>   we'll go over there and finish him off."

And this Indian, he tell 'em,

>   "Don't do that!
>   They come alive.
>   Let him come alive.
>   That's not the one that you think do it.
>   This one is from Ashnola.
>   I seen people they said he was away.
>   But he must have come down after we come by there."

They couldn't believe it.
So anyway, they tell him,

>   "If you say too much, we'll shoot you right here."

So they scared him and sent him to the camp.
Go back to where he work.

"Don't fool around.
　　Otherwise, we'll shoot you too."

So he go back to the camp.

But these white men, they go up, get up there.
Nobody with them.
Only them.
And they see the old men sit and sing his song.
And they get there.
And before they look around at the ground to see that paper,
　they don't.
Only they pull the gun on him.
And blind him again.
And shot him again.
Two, and two, three, four.
Four shots at the second time.
In the head.

And he died again.
Before they find this paper,
　stones there,
　　they should have find that first.

It mighta be different.

But they pick him up.

　　　　"Oh, this is supposed to be the chief from Ashnola.
　　　　This is his letter from Ottawa.
　　　　That is not the one they think it was.
　　　　This robber is still there in Penticton.
　　　　They never come."

So they called that—they killed him by mistake.

See?

Then they go back.
They had a boss.
There always be boss in a bunch like that.
One man.

So the boss, what they have done.
And they tell them,

      "That's not good.
        We've got to report to our headquarters,
          and see what they've got to say.
        You guys done something wrong.
        Should not do that."

Because they do that without telling him.
These are bad boys, you know.

But anyway, this time, this boss, he tell the Indian
  to go along with these others.
He sent four with that Indian there with him.
And three others.
And these two, Indian and another, they got to be together.
And these other two, they can go right by
  at the Indian camp at Ashnola.
And keep going to Osoyoos or Rock Creek, I don't know which.
That's where they had their headquarters.

So they did. They going fast. They get going
But these other two, they were together when they come.
But before they come to the Indian camp
  and the Indian and another one, they stop.
Wait 'til these two goes by.
And wait 'til they goes quite a ways by before they can get to the Indians.
And then they could tell the Indians what's going on.
Then if there's anything happens,
  just so they mighta be killed by the other Indians.
Or, they might go after these others who went away already.
One or the other, or else may not.
They kinda expect not to be trouble.
But yet, they might.
Cannot tell.

So, they wait there somewhere 'til these two goes quite a ways,
  maybe past Keremeos before these two they show up at the camp.
And they tell the Indian, said to the Indians,

      "Your chief is killed."

They missed him here but they thought he might stay there for overnight
   because there was one Indian there.
They could stay with him for overnight.
Maybe sometimes in afternoon he should come back.

But they was shot twice already before they know it.

And they told these Indians, they had that Indian interpreter,
   in Chinook.
And tell him all about.
And said to these Indians,

       "These two, they sent them to the headquarters."

That must be some kind of Indian agent or some kind of
   government man.

Then they went over there and they figure
   somebody should come from over there to see you guys.
That's the headquarters.

All right.
These Indians, they thought,

       "Well, we better wait.
         There is no use making trouble.
         Our chief is dead.
         And that's all.
         No trouble be better."

They good people.

Not like that pack horse robber.
They bad Indians.
But just a few.

So, they waited.
They could never come back that day.
Because I think that's Rock Creek.
That's too far to go on horseback
   and come back the same day.
Can't do it.
But the next day, they come,
   about five of them.

Policemen, doctor, and other government man.
And one of them, must be Indian agent.
Or maybe government man anyway.
One of these five, they give them a good talking.
They still have that Indian, they tell him,

>"You come back not tomorrow, but next day.
>And we can get here and you can come back from there.
>Then you can do the interpret.
>We going to talk to these people."

So they did.
When they come at the certain time.
And this Indian they left camp and the same one who was with him,
 and they get there.
And he was told he don't want no trouble.
He want everything to be quiet.

>"Too bad. He was killed by mistake."

So this Indian, this Indians say,

>"We agree. We can't help it.
>That's okay."

They told 'em,

>"We going to go over there, we're going to talk to this camp.
>And when we are through talking to 'em,
> we going to bring half of the bunch of pack horses
>   with the groceries on 'em,
>   and bring 'em here.
>And we take care of your death.
>And we do the cooking.
>And we do everything just like the way you do
> when somebody die.
>You tell us and we do it.
>Because ourselves, we kill that by mistake."

So that means they good friend altogether.
The camp and this other camp.

All right, they get these other five men

and that Indian from there, they all go and get to this camp.
And one of these, talk to them and they call out and tell him,

> "Take a lot of groceries and pack 'em.
> And you go over there.
> And these Indians we tell already, they comin'.
> They bring their horses. Two or three of them.
> Maybe four. They bring their horses when they get here.
> They can hand to this party and pack 'em and take 'em
>   back to the camp.
> To their camp.
> But you pack all groceries.
> And whoever, this interpreter, he can be there too.
> And he can tell the white people what they should do.
> And for two, three nights.
> And then bury the old man."

So they do that.
The other come from the camp.
But the other still there.
And they bring a lot of pack horses with the groceries.
And they get to Ashnola, they unload all this food.
And they ask the Indians what they want 'em to do.

Well, the Indians, they said,

> "That dead man has got to be buried.
> Got to dig a hole and bury him."

And the white people said,

> "Well, we do that.
> But how does you bury your people when they die?"

> "Well, we roll 'em in tule bags.
> And then we bury 'em that way."

They say,

> "All right, maybe we can do in our way.
> We can make a box.
> We can build a box in the grave when we dig the grave big.
> And deep already, six feet.

We can build a box inside, slide 'em right from the inside,
    and finish 'em.
And we can put the body in there.
But we can build the top (that will be the lid) outside here
    and then we get down and fit 'em.
And he'll be in the box buried.
That's our way."

But where do they get the box?
There is no lumber.
There is no sawmill or nothing.

But that's what they say.

So the Indians said,

     "All right, you do the way you think it should be."

All right, they go up the creek with the axe.
And they get a pole about this big, about six feet.
Cut 'em.
Bunch of them, and they carry them to the grave.
And the others, they dig a grave wide and deep.
And they put these poles.
And they build a coffin right from inside.
Right from the bottom.
Build them up about that high.
All poles.

They got nails.
They nail 'em.
And when they finish 'em in the grave, inside,
  but they make the lid a little bigger so they could fit them on top.
That'll be the lid.
More like a coffin cover.
Nowadays they make a cover.
But that just a lid.
So they finish that.
And they had the body lay there.
Was covered with good blankets, good white blankets.
For three night.
And all the Indians, they all together.

Some of them come from long ways.
And they all together.
When the time comes, they took the old man
  and put him in that box underground.
Then they put the lid on them and they nail 'em down in there.
And they bring the big stone they took out,
  they bring that alongside of 'em.
And fill that with big stone.
Then they bring light gravel and fill the grave.

That's the first Indian was on the coffin.
First one they seen him in the coffin buried.
That was in 1839.
I get that number of the year from the age, John Ashnola's age.
He's supposed to be born in 1820.
What they tell the stories and they says how old he was
  when his dad died.
That's his dad, the one that get killed up there.
So that's how I get that number.
They in 1839.
See? I go by his age and then compare to ...
  he was only something like fourteen or so.
Anyway, I know that.
So I know what number of the year.

And when they finish that and the white people stay there
  until they bury him
    in the afternoon, two o'clock.
They tell 'em, but they don't know anything about clock
  or what time in the day.
All they know is afternoon or before noon or the sun was dropping ...
  that means three o'clock.
The white people tell 'em what time, but they don't know.

See, the white people, they go watch in their pocket
  and they got watch like the one I got in my room.
They showed 'em but still they don't know.

And they bury him supposed to be at two o'clock.
And these white people stay there for that night.

And next morning when the sun was up after nine and they move out.
But the groceries, what they left, they leave 'em there.
All.
Only the horses, they take 'em back.
And the most of the Indians,
  they were very well satisfied for the thing it's done.
Not satisfied for their chief was killed,
  but satisfied killed by mistake.
And what the white people treat 'em
  that was okay.
Most of 'em agree that way.

But only four of them, something like that,
  bad people in Penticton, they not satisfied.
But they don't say nothing.
They want to hide because since that time or before that
  there was always somebody to be bad and somebody to be good.
It's always, even today.
Now today more bad than the good people.
That is now.
But those days, the bad ones not too many.
Good people is more.
Now good people is not much. Bad people is more.
Today.

So these four, they not satisfied.
But they were there.
Never said nothing.
In two, three days after that, they move the bunch from here
  up towards Princeton.
And they move as far as Five Mile (they call it).
That's supposed to be five miles from Princeton to that big creek.
And that's a great big opening just like this.
And they stop there and they stop over there for another two, three days.

And these Indians, these four,
  they know these people, they going to stop there.
They never said nothing.
At Five Mile.
And these Indians, the four Indians, they got away

and they don't go back.
They got home.
And they were bawled out by their people that were there.
No more chief, not yet.
And told 'em,

> "You should not do that.
>   That's a bad trick you done.
>   We all satisfied that way.
>   But you guys should not do it."

Oh well, they don't care.
They like to get even and kill white man.

Well, that's not good.

So that's almost to the end of that part of that stories.
In that far.

And they left.
And they keep going past Princeton.
And they keep going.
To Chilliwack.
Left their horses there
  and take the boat to Westminster and also to Vancouver, I think.
And let's see ...
  to continue that story.

Shut it off, shut it off for a while.

Harry paused for about an hour to recollect his thoughts.

At that time, that's when John Shiweelkin
  (the people call him John Ashnola, that's the name of the creek)
    but because he lives near there, that's why they call him John Ashnola.
But his right name, John Shiweelkin.
That's the son of that chief that got killed here.
And that's when he become to be chief.
They was small boy, not only him.
They got some older.
But the older says, "No, I'm not going to be chief."

And they got some younger than him.
And they said, "No, I'm too young."

John, he's kind of in the middle.
But they get him to be chief.
Ashnola.
And he was a chief ever since he die in 1918 in the month of February.
Seventh of February he die at ninety-eight years old.
Just two years under a hundred when he die.

Wendy: And didn't you spend a lot of time with him?

Oh yeah.
Yeah, I heard a lot of stories from him.
His ranch, he turn over to his son, to Pierre John.
And I work for Pierre John.
That's his dad.
So every time I get home, they always tell me stories.
Not only me but maybe somebody else too.
But I was there for quite a while.
And there's a lot of these stories he tell me.
I learned a lot of stories from him—old man John.

So that's about all for that.

You Going to Take Our Land Away from Us

A white man is murdered on the trail.

Next was the seven.
Number Seven.
Joseph Newhmkin at Chopaka.
  in 1845.
That's a long time.
1845, and he kill a white man.
And, right there at Chopaka,
  there was a church there.
And quite a few people lived there.
And Joseph Newhmkin,
  he was just about middle age at that time.
Could be around forty
  or thirty-five, something like that.
And the people, they live there,
  and they see a white man.
They seen 'em going by on the trail
  with a pack, you know,
    with a pack on his back.
But he's a white man.

And they talked about it.
And some of the Indian, they said,

> "That white man, they was told to locate our land.
> He not good.
> They locate the land.
> They going to take our land away from us."

And Joseph, they listen there.
And they think that's right.
He mad.
He think that's what the white man is going to do.

So they never said nothing.
But only the other boys that just about his age,
  and they tell them,
    they three of them,
      and they said,

> "All right, we can follow that man.
> We follow him,
>   and when we caught up to him, we kill him."

So they went on the horseback.
But this man was with a pack on foot.
But it was quite a ways behind.
Quite a while behind.
And then they went,
  near to Palmer Lake before they get there
    and then they caught up to him on the trail.
And then they tell him,

> "We kill you.
> You looking in the country.
> You white man, you going to take the land away
>   from the Indian."

But this white man, he said,

> "Well, I'm not doing that.
> I'm just going by."

But no, they did [not] believe what they think.
So they aim at the gun.
Then the white man, they blessed himself
  and they call to God.
And then they show them the God,
  but anyhow, they shot 'em.
And killed him.
And just leave 'em there.
Then they come back.
And somebody heard the shot across the valley.
Whoever lived there,
  and they was wondering what's the matter.
Who do the shooting over there?
One shot.

And the next day, they thought,

> "Maybe I better go over there and look around.
> They don't sound very good,
> that one shot."

Him and his wife, they go over there,
  just where they hear the shot.
And look around.
There was a white man lay there dead, shot.
He was shot.
So they bury 'em right there.
They dig a hole and they just throw 'em in there
  and bury 'em.
So that's what Joseph done.

> *Wendy: And that's the end of that? They never did anything*
> *to him?*

Nothing.
No law those days around here,
  no nothing.
But the people knew he did kill 'em.
He said he did.
But nobody know.
Later on, a few years after that,
  and then they become to be a chief.
He shouldn't be a chief.
See, that's the end of that story.
Joseph Newhmkin.

I'll Show Him Who's a Better Man, Him or Me

Kwol-SHASH-ket puts a trigger-happy settler in his place.

Another one,
  that's over here in Quilchena.
His name, his Indian name, Kwol-SHASH-ket.
And I don't know what that means.
That's a Thompson word.
That's in Quilchena, right in Merritt
  almost where you had a cabin there.
Just across the lake from there.

  Wendy: We went to Quilchena to see Harriet Paul last spring.

Yeah, in the lower end of Quilchena, towards Merritt.

But this one here I was going to tell you—
  on the lower end of that lake, towards Merritt,
    the time we moved your stuff to that cabin.
And just about straight across the lake from there.
Right by the highway now.
There was a nice little place up the creek—
  there was kind of a creek from the mountain.
Small creek.
And a white man take that land for his land.
He build a cabin there.
And he lived there.
Big man.
White man.
Tall and big.
Strong man.
And mean.

And he take that land
  and he put in a garden, any garden, you know,

vegetables, potatoes, tomatoes and things like that.
Just garden.
The road was between his fence and the lake.
Was the road.
Same place where the highway is now.
But at that time just the train or just the wagon road.
Then,
  he raise the garden on the upper side of the road
    then he works there,
      sometimes he works there,
        he gonna garden, you know.

Then some of the Indians they movin' by there with the pack horses
  and they got some dogs, just like Rufus [Wendy's dog] ... (*laughs*)
And, you know, a bunch of Indians movin' along.
And maybe two, three dogs, you know, each one, they had a dog.
And the dogs were runnin'.
You know how it is with dogs, that they can go under the fence.
Then they go in the garden,
  then they run around and they make damage you know, in the garden.
And that white man, he really mad.
Then he gets a stone and throw it at the dog and hit it and hurt it.
And somebody tell 'em,

     "Here, don't hit my dog with the rock."

     "Ah," he says, "I'll down you too!"

So, you know, everybody is scared of him.
He's a tall man, big.
And he got a mustache, nothing like this—
  a beard right down to here.

And finally they, so many people go by there with the dog
  and always the dog goes in the garden.

And he pick up a gun, a small gun, like a 22,
  there is no 22 that time, they call it 25 Stephenson.
The bullet was this size.
That's what they kill the grouse.
They had one of 'em.
And he took that

and he leave it there when he work.
Whenever a dog or somebody go by with a dog
  and if the dog runs that way,
    even if he don't make no damage or nothin',
      he pick up the gun and shoot the dog and kill them.

Or they cripple 'em.
They wounded, like,
  and then the dog maybe not die,
    but he's hit and crippled.
But some of them, they hit 'em in the right spot and he killed them.
Nothin' you can do about it because he's strong man.
And the people don't like that—even the white people.
He do that to everyone, you know.
He's mean.

And that Kwol-SHASH-ket, just a small man.
About middle build, not too big not too small.
But he's smaller than that white man anyway.
So he heard that.
People talked about that white man,

    "He's bad, mean."

So Kwol-SHASH-ket, he says,

    "Now, whenever you Indians movin' there
      and I can go along.
      And take your dogs along."

And he tell the Indians, that white man, they tell the Indians,

    "When you go by there with your dog,
      before you get to here and pick up your dog
        and tie him with a rope and then you lead him.
    You lead him to go by here.
    ·When you gets far away then turn 'em loose.
    You can always lead him, tie him up and lead him.
    That way I never kill them.
    But if you let him loose I will shoot him."

So the Indians or white people they know that.
Before they get there, they pick up the dog

and tie him with a rope and lead him to go by there.
Then turn 'em loose.

Well they can't do that all the time.
That's not good, you know.
That's no way to do.
Kwol-SHASH-ket, he says,

> "Now, we move that way.
> I go along.
> Take your dogs along.
> Let him do something with the dog.
> I'll show 'em who's a better man, him or me."

They say,

> "All right."

But the Indian, he know he was pretty strong.
He know that.

So they movin' along.
They got some dogs.
Then the dogs, they went over there
  and then they scratch you know, makin' damage on the garden.
And by God that man he pick up the gun
  and Kwol-SHASH-ket, they get off the horse
    and he says,

> "Here, don't shoot the dog!"

And he look and,

> "The hell with you!"

And Kwol-SHASH-ket, he go through the fence,
  not a wire fence, a wooden fence, rails, you know.
Go over the fence.

And he says,

> "Don't come over the fence.
> This is my land, this side of the fence.
> Don't come over."

Kwol-SHASH-ket, he says,

> "This is my land too, not you.
> This is my land."

They go over.
And he went over there and he turned around with the gun.
And Kwol-SHASH-ket tell 'em,

> "Shoot if you want to shoot."

And he kept a-comin' but he don't shoot.
But he point the gun to him but he never shoot.
And Kwol-SHASH-ket, he kept a-coming.
And they pointed the gun to him but they don't fire.
And Kwol-SHASH-ket he kept a-comin' and he grab the gun
  and pull out of his hands,
    just take it like that.
And throw the gun over the fence.
Then he started moving his hand, he's going to hit like that.
Just catch his arm and just pull him that way
  and over they went with his legs you know, up and down.
And Kwol-SHASH-ket jump on him and he sit on his chest.
And he put his knees in both arms.
Then they grabbed the beard here (*laughs*).
And he hit 'em with his head, you know.
Grab 'em here.
Beard, you know.
Then they grabbed him there.
Then he slap 'em pretty hard.
And he hollered and he says,

> "Leave me alone. I give up."

He says,

> "You've got to give up.
> If you don't give up I can kill you if I wanted to.
> I can kill you right there.
> You pick up the gun.
> You think you're going to shoot me.
> If you shoot me, you think the gun is going to go

into my body.
It never will."

So the white man, he got no more to say.

So Kwol-SHASH-ket told him,

    "You've got to be a good man from now on.
    Don't do that anymore.
    Even if I'm not along here,
     if you do that somebody will tell me.
    Then I can come and I'll fix you worse than now.
    Or else I can kill you.
    If you don't want that kind of way, move out of here.
    Go up on the hillside somewhere
     where there's no people around,
    In the lonely place,
     then you can make a garden there,
      and nobody can come around with a dog,
       that is, if you don't want that,
        get out of here.
    Otherwise don't do that again if you stay here.
    From now on don't do that.
    I'm going to fix you next time."

Well, the white man, he can tell because they couldn't handle him.
They only small man, smaller than him.

No more!
He don't do that no more.
He don't like it but he wouldn't do it
  because he's scared of Kwol-SHASH-ket.

When he find out, he's going to get it.

So he's there for about another two years.
Then he go away.
They moved somewhere.
No more.
So that Kwol-SHASH-ket—
  the Indians find out he was a really strong man.
And he stopped the fights—
  sometimes people fight—

then he go over there and stop them.
Nobody can do anything with him
  because they knew he was a really strong man.

But he's not mean.
He's a good man.
But there's nothing can do anything about him, you know.

I KILL HIM BECAUSE HE'S TRYING TO FORCE ME

A woman travelling alone confronts her attacker.

And, there's an Indian lady.
Her name Madeleine.
And, Madeleine Shkoo-WOWT-kin , that was her name.
And she was going along,
  all alone on a foot,
    walking.

> *Wendy: Was this a long time ago?*

That's a long time ago.

> *Wendy: A hundred years? 1800s?*

I could not tell.
That lady, I seen her,
  she was very old.
Pretty close to ninety when I seen 'em.
About ninety.

> *Wendy: And how old were you then?*

I was eighteen at that time.

> *Wendy: So that was around 1918?*

She died in 1918 in November,
  in month of November.
But she's pretty old.
Could be about ninety,
  or maybe eighty-five,
    or something like that.
But she done that when she was thirty years old,
  or forty.

They met a man, white man.
They met them
  and they were walking on the road
    on the trail.
So, somehow they kill that man.
They kill 'em with a knife.
Cut 'em.

  Wendy: Why?

Well, the way they were saying,
  this man was trying to force 'em.
So they kind of fight back.
They got a knife
  and the first thing they know,
    they cut 'em with a knife
      and then they cut 'em bad.
And this white man, they died.
And they just leave 'em there
  and then they come.

So, in a few days and somebody go by
  and then they see this white man
    laying dead.
Must've been died after two, three days.
They never said nothing when she come.
They never said, "Did she kill a man?"
They never said nothing.
But, the other people,
  they were saying that Madeleine,
    at that time they left from here
    and then they go that way.
It kind of look,
  that was the time they killed that white man.
They got the idea that way.
So finally, the chief, they asked 'em
  and then they kind of scared
    and they tell 'em,

        "If you don't say the truth,
          we going to tie you up
            and we going to hang you alive."

Tie the legs and the feet
  and then hang them.
They got to tell.
You know, they get them in the corner.
So finally they said,

    "Yeah, I killed him all right."

So these other people from where they come, you know,
  like from Indian Edward's place,
    and they were the bunch, they found this man,
      lay there.
And then they bury him.
But they thought, could be her done that.
But not sure.
Because they know they left there
  and looks like the same time
    because this man when they was found,
      they'd been dead about two days.
So the chief, they just scared her, you know.
They tell 'em,

      "If you don't say the truth,
          we could tie you hands and your legs
              and we going to hang you 'til you say the truth."

So they say,

      "Yeah, I kill 'em.
          Because they trying to force me,
            that's why I kill 'em.
          I get so mad, the first thing I knew,
          I cut 'em badly already.
          But he was still alive and I left him there.
          They must've died after I left."

So that's all there is for that story.
Madeleine, they kill a man.
She kill a man.

    Wendy: She had good reason to kill him.

Oh yeah.
And then, that way they never—
  of course those days, you know,
    they never report 'em to the court or anything like that.
They just leave it as they are.

THE WHITE PEOPLE MAKE MONEY OUT OF HIM

A Similkameen man is secretly abducted from prison.

And another one,
  that would be the three.
This is a big man,
  not *really* big,
    but anyways kinda tall
      and nobody know he's very strong.
But he was.
And over there in Kaleden, now they call 'em,
  not Kaleden—Okanagan Falls.
That's where the Indians gather, getting the salmon.
The salmon come up the river
  and then they get there to that dam.
    where that dam is now.
It was a dam long long time.
Coyote build that dam.
But since, the white people put some cement to it
  and raise it up.
But it was a dam long long time.
The salmon never go by there.
They can come as far as there.
No more.
Because the water was falling.
And that's where the Indians gets together
  And gets salmon
They stay there ten days or so, you know, and then get out of there.
And this time when the Indians were there
  and some of them get the salmon
    and some of them go up in the hillside and hunt.
Some of them play stick game and so on, you know.
  play cards and stick game.
And some Indians they play, and they, horse to horse.

If one of them lose, he lose his horse.
And the other one win that horse.
They play that way.
They play cards.
Horse to horse.
Then, the one of them, they win that horse.
And whoever they own that horse,
  and they said to the other one,

> "You not win that, you cheat me.
>   If you didn't cheat, you wouldn't win.
>   But you win all right by cheatin'. You cheat me."

> "No," the other one said,
> "No I didn't cheat you. I just got you beat.
>   You just lose, that's all."

> "No."

They want to take that horse back.
So this other one, the one that win that horse,
  wouldn't let him take it.
But he want to take it.
So they grabbed the rope.
And the other one grabbed the same rope and the same rope.
And then they pull, you know,
  whoever gets the rope, all the rope too,
    well, that's his horse.
Should be.
That's the way they figure.
Then they pull the rope.

And this other one—
  his name Newhmkin.
And he went over there.
And he said,

> "Yeah, you fellas you better stop.
>   That man, he win that horse, he's not cheatin'.
>   You just too crooked.
>   You think he's cheatin'.
>   They not cheatin'.
>   You lose."

"Oh no. I'm going to take my horse back."

Well, Newhmkin told 'em,

"You just watch, whether you take it back or not."

Newhmkin turned around and he hit the horse right in the ribs.
With his (*claps*)
  with his hand.
He hit it right in the rib.
And the horse just fall down.
And knocked out.

And he let go, let go of the rope, the both of 'em.
Because their horse were fall and dead.
Looks like he's dead.
But they're knocked out.

After a while the horse was just shake there.
And he got up again.

And who's going to hit the horse with his hand?
The horse he knocked out.
You can't.
You can't even do that on the dog.
Maybe you can on the cat, but not on the dog.
Not on the horse.
But Newhmkin, he just give 'em one hit
  then the horse just drop.
And that shows he's strong, he's got the power.
But he's not mean. He's a good boy.

And that was my grandfather.
My mother's dad, that guy.
So since that time everybody know he's quite a guy.
He's strong.

And the one fella,
  they call him George,
    George Jim, his name was.
George Jim, he's ... he's kind of outlaw.
He's a bad man, mean.
He can fight.

He's strong, big man.
Not tall but kind of big stout man.
He's good fighter.
He's pretty strong.
And he's kind of mean.
He always like to fight
  because when he fight he beat somebody.
And this time there at the Okanagan Falls
  when they gettin' the salmon,
    and one of the Shuttleworth
      (Shuttleworth is half-Indian and half-white),
And they were drinkin.'
Somehow they kind of fight, you know.
And George, he beat that Harry Shuttleworth.
He beat 'em and he pretty near killed him.
And somebody goin' to stop them
  and nobody could stop George
    because he strong man.
And then Newhmkin, they were out there somewhere
  and then somebody told him
    they were fighting over there
      and George is trying to kill that Harry.

He said,

      "Maybe I better go and see 'em."

So they went over there and he was still hittin' him.
Harry was down and pretty near dead.
And George was still kick him or hit 'em with his hand.
And Newhmkin get there,
  and he says,

      "George."

And he look.

Says,

      "You better stop. Don't kill that man."

And George, he says,

"It's not your business."

And Newhmkin never said nothing.

And he grab him (he's got a coat on).
He grab him by the neck.
Pull him and he throw him *way* over.
And he fall on his back.
And then his legs was up.
They were lay there for a while.
Kinda knocked out
  'cause he landed on the ground so hard
    by pull him and throw him.
Then stop.
And when he got up, and told him,

"Don't you go over there."

So he stop.
He know how strong, who throw him.
So that twice Newhmkin, they do that.

But that man, that Harry he's still alive.
They kicked him in the ribs and broke the ribs.
They beat him.
Just pretty near dead.
And he still lived.
That was the month of September.
And Harry was livin'
  'til sometimes in February the next year.
And then he died that way—by beatin' by George.

Then, George, the police was goin' to get him.
But the policeman were afraid,
  afraid of him
    because they knew he was pretty strong and mean.
And they figured they going to cheat them somehow.
Then catch him.
But he's too smart.
He wouldn't let the policeman men catch him.
One year after, that man died.
He killed that man you know,

not right away but he died that way by beatin'.
And finally some smart man—they get him all right—
    they call 'em these days, you know, the road gang,
        like the road construction.
They had a camp, those days.
Camp someplace and then they work on the road with the horses,
    no equipment like they have now—
        just the horses and plow.
And scrape with the hand, hand scraper they used.
They gotta have a camp someplace.
And where they had the camp, there was a cook house.
And they board there.
And one of them, one of the bosses like,
    they went from the other side of Keremeos
        about sixteen, seventeen miles below
            just where they had the camp.
And this man went over the hill to Fairview.
Fairview was a little town on the west side from Oliver—mine town—
    small little town.
But there's policemen there
    and the court and everything.
No town where Oliver is now, that time.
But only Fairview.
One of these bosses they have to go over there.
And then the government office is there, you know.
Then when he go back
    and they happen to run into George Jim,
Met him on the Spotted Lake.
There somewhere.
They met him there
    and then they went together.
And it was towards supper time
    and they go.
And 'bout six o'clock
    and all they workers they get back to the camp—
        ready to eat.
And this man, he says to George,

> "You better come, come with me
>   and then supper time, and then you eat there.
>   And after you eat then you go."

157

Everybody knows he's outlaw.
And this man they had to figure you know—
  he might catch him,
    because there was a reward to him—
I think it was $250.
Those days, you know, everything is cheap—
Whoever catch him, they can get that money—
So George he didn't want to go.
You know, he's smart.
So this man tell 'em,

    "You better come."

He says,

    "No I don't want to go."

    "Nobody will do anything to you.
      You come and you eat.
      After supper and then you go."

So finally, they must have been hungry.
So they go over there.
And because George they could not understand in English,
  they can understand in Chinook, some, not all.
When they get there
  and a lot of men they're mixed you know.
And I guess the man, they tell the others,

    "That's the outlaw.
      We going to get him somehow."

And one of the workers they get the apron,
  like my apron.
They get that
  and put 'em on over the shoulders, you know.
Looks like a cook.
That's not a cook.
That's one of the workin' mans.
Then, the table in the tent—
  you know, the two table—
    the long one, one that way and the other one this way
      inside the tent.

And this new cook,
  they carried the food in a dish
    and set it on the table along.
And they goes to the stove
  and they bring some more
    and they set it.
Looks like it's a cook—
  and they told George, the other one told him,

        "You sit here."

They don't want to sit there.
They figure they should sit close to the tent
  so his back can be towards the tent.
But the other people they sit there and they tell him,

        "Here, there's room here.
          You sit here."

That's in the middle, like,
  so the waiter can go by on his back, you know,
    to go by that way.
So they figure that way.
So finally he sit there
  and he eat
    and the waiter goes by to his back,
      back and forth
        get some food.
And come back.
And by this time they get a club
  and they hide it, you know.
And George, he didn't know that when they go by.
And they hit him in the head, hard.
And George just drop off from the chair
  and knocked out.
And then everyone they sit on him.
And then some of them get the rope
  and tie their hands,
    tie them in this way.
And then got him.
And then when he come to, he's already tied,
  his hands are this way.

Then they keep him.
Then they sent one guy to get the policeman
  because the policeman come.
When they come they're going to handcuff him.
He's gotta be handcuffed because he killed a man.
If he can't go now he'll go in the morning

Then they got George
  and they send him, they take him to Penticton
    and they had trial then.
And then they take him to Vernon.
And they have trial there.
That's the high court.
Then they trial there a few times
  and then he got the sentence—seven years,
    sentenced seven years to be in jail.
So they sent him to Westminster in the penitentiary.
And he was there three years, three years in jail.
And then that George Jim, he belong right here at Ashnola.
That's where his dad live.
And they got a ranch and that's his people.
That's Ashnola man.
So they send the word, send a letter.
Those days, you know, the mail carrier on the saddle horse.
They send a letter from Westminster to these people
  and tell them,

        "That relative of yours, that George Jim,
            he died.
          They got sick and died."

Just to let them know.
They bury 'em there.
But these people, Indians,
  thought they should go over and get him,
    even after he's buried.
Dig him out and bring him, bury him here.
So they do.
They went and get there.
And then they said,

        "We want that man, the one who died.

We gonna get him out and take him home
and bury him over there."

White people tell them,

"All right, but you don't have to dig him.
We'll do that.
We can dig him out
  and we'll change the coffin, and seal it.
But don't open it.
Because it's not good. Already bad, you know.
Rotten.
So take him."

So they wait for the white people.
They don't go over there.
But the white people dig and put him in a box,
  a new box.
And sealed it so nobody can open it.
And told them not to open it.

"That's him all right but don't open it.
It's not good.
It could smell, not open."

They bring him from Westminster on a boat as far as Hope.
Then when they left their horses at Chilliwack
  because they got some feed there.
And anyway they, some of them gettin' off from the boat at Chilliwack
  and bring the horses.
But maybe one of them come with the body as far as Hope.
And unload him from the boat.
And they bring the horses and pack them on the horse
And bring them over the trail
  and get them back to Ashnola.
They think that it was him.
But the other people it's there—at home, they say,

"We can open take a look."

Well, all these other people
  that went over there to get him say,

"We was told not to open it."

They say,

>"Never mind.
> because you go over there that far to get him.
> But we can see. Maybe not him.
> We better see."

All right, they chop the coffin and they open it
  and they looked at him.
It wasn't George.
He's a Chinaman.
It's not a very big man.
George is a big stout man,
  but this Chinaman is just a small man.
And they can tell it's a Chinaman.
He died not long.
That's a different one.
That's too bad.
Then they for a while,
  and they thought maybe they mistake from over there.
They went back,
They buried this Chinaman there.
When they get back to Westminster then they told in jail,

>"The one we took from here,
> he's not George.
> That's a Chinaman.
> We opened 'em."

>"Well, all right," they said,
>"we mistake.
> After you guys were gone
> and then we find out we did mistake,
> George is there.
> That's Chinaman all right.
> Now we dig 'em out and you take it home."

The second time done the same way,
  the same thing.
And they do the same way

and they bring him.
On the second time they get them there at home,
  still the others told 'em,

> "Open him.
>   We'll take a look."

Then they open him and there was a Negro boy.
It's not George!

And George, he said,
  when he met the other Indian in England
    and he said to him,
      this other Indian his name is Charlie,
        Charlie Harvey, his name was.
He was an Indian from Enderby.
But he was in the army.
He's a half-white and half-Indian.
And he was in the army and he get to England.

Then the boys, the army boys with him
And this army boys,
  they told him,

> "Not far from here
>   there was an Indian there,
>   he's supposed to be from Canada.
>   Maybe we'll take you over there and see,
>   maybe you know 'em.
>   He's supposed to be coming from Okanagan."

Well, Enderby, they speak in Okanagan, you know.

So Charlie, he said,

> "Maybe the government might not like it
>   that way to go and see him."

> "Ah never mind. The government they wouldn't know.
> We take you over there.
> We don't have to tell the government."

So they take him over there and they showed him.
He's living in one place

and they ask whoever they look after him,
  and they said,

     "All right you can see 'em."

So they stay and he talk in his language.
That's George.
And Charlie asks him,

     "How come for you to be here in England?"

     "Well," he says,
     "I was in Westminster in jail, three years.
      One, morning—two o'clock in the morning—
        three policemen come in.
      The door was locked, but they got the key
       and they opened 'em with their key,
        three policemen.
      Three of them come in at two o'clock in the morning
       and tell they me 'get up and brush up.'"

They got different clothes in jail,
The jailer got different clothes.
But they give him different clothes, good clothes.

     "Here put these clothes on we wait here for you.
      We take you. We move you.
      You in jail here but we take you to east
       long way from here.
      There was another jail.
      That's where you're going to be,
       from now the rest of your time
        to be in jail.
      Move you."

Well what he got to say?
He's in jail
  and the policeman told him in the morning, early.
So he put that clothes on
  and take him on the buggy to Vancouver.
And then wait there awhile and then in the morning,
  I don't know what time the train goes out from Vancouver to East.
And they put him in there and then these policemen,

the three of them, they all get in the train.
And they took him East on the train.

When they get far away somewhere in halfways
  near Winnipeg or somewhere in there.
And they go in the dining room in the train
  the policemen,
    and they took George over there to eat.
When the policemen get through eatin'
  and they go back to where they was, you know.
But George he still there and eat.
And nobody there but him.
And then the waiter come
  and ask him, he said,

       "Do you know where you're going?"

He said,

       "No. I supposed to go somewhere this way,
         supposed to be another jail
           where I'm going to be.
       I was in jail over there in British Columbia."

And this man, this is the waiter, told him,

       "When you get far away you will stop someplace,
         wait for the boat.
       You might stay there three or four days, maybe more.
       They might keep you in jail,
         or keep you someplace so you wouldn't get away.
       Then when the boat comes,
         and they going to put you in the boat.
       Then you're going to cross the oversea.
       That's where they take you."

They tell him that much and somebody come.
No more.

So finally the first thing they knew
  they were over there in Halifax there somewhere.
Wait there for a few days
  and then they go on the boat.

And told him,

      "We got to go on the boat for some distance
      but go over the sea."

The first thing he knew he was in England.
And they kept him there, not in jail—
  one good house, one good room—
    just himself in there.
But they always watch him.
Once in a while they take him out,
  take him on the train or a stage—
    they call 'em those days—horses.
Take him away.
Some other town in some other places—
  they took him France, took him in Germany, Yugoslavia,
    all those places, for two—three months.
Then come back.
The same place.
That's his home, like—
But stay there for a month or more
  and then take him away.
All over in European he been.
So, they take him in one place—
  great big building.
They put 'em in there and then all the people go in there,
  they have to pay,
    pay money to see the Indian.

      "That's the Indian from the Indian land.
      That's from here."

Because over there they never see Indian.
So the other people, they make money out of him over there.
And the other people has to pay money to see him.
And he knew, all the people knew he was an outlaw.

So when Charlie come back from England
  and he get back to Enderby.
And George told him,

      "When you get back, you go to Ashnola
      and tell my uncle and tell my aunt,

                they got lots of money,
                    they got a lot of cattle,
                        they got a lot of money.
        They should try to get me back home.
        You can tell them
            they should contact to the Indian Affairs
                in Ottawa, Indian agent round there.
        They can do the help to Ottawa
            and then whoever is going to come and get me,
                their fare, they going to be paid from the Indian money."

He told them that.

But Charlie come back.
One year after he come back,
    and he ride over saddle horse
        and get to Ashnola
            and told the people there.
And he told all of what he was saying.
But these Indian they could not understand.
They don't know what to do to get over there.
That's too far.
They not understanding.
And Charlie told them,

            "I can go with you people.
            I can go with you people   ·
                to do the talking
                    because you can't understand."

But him, you know, he can talk in English and in Indian.
But still they don't go.
But they know George is over there.
He didn't die.
So finally after that he might have died then but nobody know.

They seems to be stealed him.

So that's the one.
Now maybe ...
I'm suposed to tell you George.
I suppose to finish that.
That is the way I tell the story.

A lot of time I kinda tell something
  then I kinda switch to another one.
I couldn't help it, I gotta tell that.
That way it takes longer.
But that's a kind of important story anyway.

That's one thing the white people
  have done to the Indian is not good.

The way they say,
  that George Jim is kinda funny-looking man.
You never see that kind of person.
They say he was big.
Not tall,
  not too tall.
But he was kinda big and stout
  and his face was all different
And he got a big head.
Kinda funny-looking man.
But he's strong, and he's outlaw.
So that's why, I guess, they kept him.
In another way he's a murderer.
Supposin' if they let him out in seven years,
  they might do that again.
So in that case they keep him that way
  so he wouldn't do that anymore.
And the white people make money out of him.
  for a long time.

So we leave that.

WILD HORSES, THEY KILL 'EM

*Harry recalls the days of wild horses
in the Similkameen Valley.*

At that time, there was fences at that border.
And the loose horses, lots of 'em.
And, no oats in those days.
Nothin'.
Nothin' but bunchgrass.
No sagegrass, just the bunchgrass.
And no town, nothin' there.
Just two, three buildings.
There was somebody who lived there along the lake,
  they just a few people.
And we used to go right to the border where the fence was,
  and a lot of horses.
And we chased 'em.
They real wild horses.
They can run.
Just like a deer.
And our saddle horses, they can run too.
And maybe three, four of us, right to the border.
And then we chased the horses.
But the other two, three, at the foothills.
They wait there.
And we run from the border 'bout—oh, four miles—
  somethin' like that.
We run pretty fast.
Chase the horses.
'Til we come to the foothills.
Then we stop.
And then these others they're waitin' there,
  they chase the horses up the hill.
Not too far—about a mile.

And they get up to the top.
And then there was another bunch there.
On top.
And then these others stopped there.
And we stopped.
And this next bunch, the third bunch,
  they chased the horses,
    on the level like that.
They come 'round the Spotted Lake,
  and they come 'round the mountain.
But we come on the road, slow.
And we get on that side, towards Richter Pass,
  then we meet these horses.

We kind of watch 'em.
When they come round the hill,
  and we go from hill,
    and we scare them.
And down it went in the valley at the Richter Pass.
And then we get together and we chase the horses
  right to the Similkameen River.
Then we cross the river and we put them right where the church is now.
And they got a big yard and a big corral and we put them all—
  bunch of horses, maybe sixty, seventy, maybe eighty horses.
Some of them with brand on them belongs to someone.
And some of them, no brand.
And whoever owns these horses, they pick 'em up.
Then some of them pick up, some they pick up some of the horses
  for himself.
That's for his work, you know, chasing horses.
Then we chasing horses there for about two weeks every year.
A lot of fun, chasin' horses.

But that was all over.

One time, the government people come around
  and they shoot the horses.
They shoot 'em right on the range.

  Wendy: Why?

Too many horses.

170

They figure that they goin' to run the cattle on the range.
But they got too many horses.
And nobody own these horses.
Just the wild horses.
So they kill 'em.
They shoot 'em.
The government do that.
And they got some cowboys to go out on the range to shoot the horses.
They had quite a lot of trouble about.
Some of them, there's quite a few got shot,
    man, you know, by the other man.
Because they shouldn't be another man's horses.
Then somehow they hidin' somewhere
    and when they ridin' by, they shot 'em.
It happened that way in Williams Lake.
Two or three men got killed that way.
That's the horse shooter.
But anyway, they get rid of a lot of horses.

Picked Up by a Big Bird

A hunter is picked up by a large bird
and deposited on a high ledge.

There was a bunch of men,
  about four men,
    they were hunting.
That's over in the Kootenay someplace.
That's way over in the east.
I don't know just where.
I think it's around—
  it's around Arrow Lake somewhere there.
And these four men
  they went hunting.
And they went up on the hill,
  on the mountains
    and they stopped
      and they say
        maybe one of them can go up higher.
And the other one can go kind of low,
  and these other two can go that way
    and there was kind of a little ridge.
Just a narrow ridge
  it's a long ridge
    it's just a narrow.
And the other one can go on that side
  and one of them can follow that ridge.
That's what they say.
And when they get up to the top somewhere,
  then they'll get together.
So they split out.
And they went hunting.
And this man, this one he goes on that narrow ridge—
  the ridge is kind of curved, like,

crooked ridge—
   but it's ridge for a long ways
     it's kind of narrow.
On that side.
And they could see
  the one of 'em, it's lower,
   and the other one is on top, like.
So this man,
  he was going along that ridge.
And this other one there watching him.
They could see him that far,
  could be about half-mile
   that they could still see 'em.
Then they hear the ...
  sounds like a wind,
   wind blowing or something.
Then they just looked around,
  they don't know which ...
   where they come from,
    but they just heard 'em
     in the air.
But soon they could see a big bird,
  great, big bird, they were flying
   towards that man that was climbing on the narrow ridge.
And this one, the one that climbs on the ridge
  and they stopped.
And the other man they watching.
And they looked around,
  and they must be doesn't know what ...
   what was what—
    no plane those days, that's a long time ago.
But this bird, they're flying
  and they just pretty near touched the ridge
   and then they pick him up
    by the feet, you know.
Picked him up,
  and then this other one, they was watching him
   when the bird
    they pick up the man and
     up they goes
      and raise 'em and fly.

Fly to the north, northwest, I think.
Yeah—they fly toward northwest.
They watch 'em fly that way.
They know they were picked up.
They were watching him.

So this man they picked up,
 they never got hurt,
  they still all right.
But the bird was holding him.
And the bird fly.
And they fly
 for a long ways in the daytime, you know,
  before noon.
And they watched,
 they see all the country,
  they knew which way they were going.
And they fly for a long ways.
Getting to be in the afternoon,
 could be somewhere around
  four or five o'clock in summertime, you know.
So they landed in one place
 and then they could see that man,
  they could see that there was a bluff
   right around,
    high, pretty high
     but the top is, it's a big ground,
      they got some trees
       and little holes, and
        big ones.
They see that from a long ways,
 just like you was going in a plane, you know.
They could see.
But they landed there.
And when they landed down there, they let them go.
And the bird it just walked a little ways
 and stopped and sit there.
And this man, they never got hurt.
Nothing wrong with 'em—they walked.

So they could see that bluff right around.
They thought maybe some place it might be kind of

kind of open,
  they might go down that way
    to make it.
So they go right around
  edge of the bluff
    for quite a ways.
Go right around,
  they never find anywhere that—
    they can't jump, it's too high—
      they can't jump, it's too high, like.
They might find some ...
  some other way kind of way,
    but they couldn't go
      maybe they can jump for some, you know
        but they couldn't find anywhere.
Just nothing but bluff clean around
  for quite a ways.

So they can't get away.
So he thinks he's going to—
  he's going to stay there 'til he dies
    if they can't get away.
They can't jump, they too high.
They walked around,
  and they walked around,
    they looked around.
And this bird just stopped there
  and they sit there, and they put—
    they big one!—
      they put their head over
        in their wing there,
          and they sleep.

They go over there and get near
  they looked at him ...
    great, big bird.
So they go to some directions a little ways
  and then they can see all kinds of bones.
Deer bones,
  bear,
    and any kind of bone, you know,
      maybe coyote or something

that he must have picked them up and
    bring 'em
        and he must have eat them.
Then they put them in one place
  all the bones.
There's lot of bones,
  they must have been doing that for a long time.
Some [of] the bones were very old,
  some kind of fresh.
Mostly deer bone and the bear.

So they thinks
  that's what they're going to do with me,
    they're going to eat me,
        then they're going to put me here on this bunch of bones.
Only my bones.
They thought,
  I'm going to kill 'em.
    And he's going to die before me.

So they went back and
  they got some rope.
Around his waist you know, they got the rope
  in case if they kill a deer,
    they might tie him with that rope
        and drag him.
That's why they have the rope around the waist.

And ...
  that's what he thought,
    they thought he's going to kill 'em.
Before he die,
  because he know he's going to die there,
    he's got no way to get out of there.
But that bird, they can fly away.
So they thought they can kill the bird
  and then the bird can die
    before him.

So they went over there,
  and they get a big long club, you know,
    a stick about so big

just so they can hit him in the head with that.
So the bird was sleeping.
So they take that pole
  and they walked over there and they
    poked him a little, kind of
      so they could take their head out, you know,
        because they had him under the wing,
          like that.
So they raise their head,
  and they hit him right in the head.

  Harry slaps his hands.

And they just kept hitting him until ...
  'til they knock him down
    and they kept hitting him and they
      smashed their head and they,
        they kill him.

Then it's not too far from the edge of the bluff.
But the bluff is high.
So they looked around,
  they thought they got that rope
    and they thought they going to find some poles.
A long pole they could stretch out the wings.
The bird wings,
  they could stretch 'em right out.
And then they,
  they did stretch 'em out and then they
    got the idea how long the pole they going to get.
And they get the pole
  and they stretch the wings of that bird.
And they tied him on the pole with the rope, you know.
They tied him and they
  stretch, like that.
But there's a pole, you know,
  right on his back.
So they dragged him
  to the edge of the bluff.
Right to the edge,
  and then they ride him.
They ride him on his back, and then they,

they raise him.
Then they thought if they'd raise him just about
  in the balance,
    then they going to kick the ground and let him fly.
But he's dead.
But the wing, it's stretched out.
They figure they,
  they might not go too fast,
    not drop, maybe.
So they did.
Then they raise him
  just about on the balance
    and then they kicked the ground,
      and away they goes
        over the bluff.
And they balance it you know,
  it's going to go too much that way and then they
    put his weight this way and then they
      too much this way and then they
        go that way.
They kept doing that 'til ...
  'til they pretty near get to the bottom.
And the bottom is not bad—
  no rocks, but it's
    some trees.
They thought they going to miss the tree.
But never, they—they go right to the tree
  and then they
    got hanged on the top of the tree.
And then finally
  they grab on the tree and then they
    change to the tree,
      but the bird was twisted, like,
      and then
        fall the other way.
But he come down on the tree
  he never got hurt or nothing,
    he's all right.
And he got down to the bottom.
But it's a long ways,
  but they knew which way they come

when the bird was carrying them and they ...
    they placed the place, you know,
        they know which way they'll have to go back.

And these others,
    they seen him picked up by the bird.
And they watchin' which way they go,
  'til they go out of the sight.
So they go back
  to the camp, you know,
    to where there's a lot of people.
And they told the people,

       "This is what happens with our friend."

So they get together and they said,

       "We have to go and look for him.
       They might be someplace.
       They might [have] dropped him.
       If you know the direction of which way they go,
         we go that way to see if we can find him."

So the bunch of 'em,
  maybe five or six,
    and then they went that way.
But this man,
  when they get down to the bottom
  and then they knew which way to go.
It's in the jackpine, you know,
  all jackpine and little,
    little mountains.
So finally they,
  they, because [his] gun you know,
    when they
      picked him up with that bird and then they
        dropped his gun—you know,
          nothing to carry.
But these others,
  they got the gun.
And then they come and
  they fire a shot once in a while.

just in case they might be alive.
If they dropped him, they
  might be alive ...
    might be hurt,
      but might be alive.
They might hear the fire shot, you know,
  and then they might holler, or something,
    or might make a smoke.
So they did.
They got matches.
That's not long ago, you know.
They got matches and those days,
  they got the gun already.
So they make a fire, and they make a smoke.
So these people who they looking for,
  they can see a smoke long ways.
So they thought
  that would be him,
    he might be alive yet.
So they go straight to that.
So finally, they,
  they find 'em.
They fire a shot,
  these other boys.

But they got no gun to fire a shot, you know.
They make a smoke
  and they holler.
So finally they could hear somebody holler
  and they just go over there
    in the jackpine.
Thick jackpine.
But they get 'em,
  they find 'em.
And they took him home.
He was all right.
They didn't get hurt.

So that's the end of the story about that.
Supposed to be big bird.
Great, big bird.
They fly

and there was supposed to be a little ridge,
  another ridge up the hill, like,
    and then they walking on the ridge.
And then the other guy from across the gully, like,
  quite a ways
    and they could hear that when they flew,
      they make a lot of noise,
        sounds like a big wind.
And then they see the bird was flying,
  and they watch his,
    his friend.
And the bird go by,
  and they pick him up.
And the bird went—
  so that's how they know.
There was a big bird.

And when I was in—I was in Ottawa one time,
  and I go to a museum.
And I seen the ...
  supposed to be bird's leg from the knees here,
    and up here,
      that's the upper leg only.
Eight feet long.
And the joint is about this big
  in both ends, you know.
And the centre of the,
  of the upper leg was about this big.
But it's written there,
  it's supposed to be a bird's leg.
So that could be the bird I guess,
  that been flying around, maybe.
That's the way I knew about this story.

I think that's all. You shut it off.

  Harry paused for a few minutes.

So then they can prove it was a big bird around at one time.
The Indians
  a long time—
    well, not too long—

can be about [a] hundred years ago
      and the Indians, they go to
         Loomis, you know Loomis,
            you go by there.
The other side of Loomis,
   and there was a little mountain,
      kind of little peak—
         it's kind of high, though.
But it's kind of narrow peak.
And the Indians
   they had a camp in
      in the bottom of that point.
Spring water there.
They put in a camp and then they
   digging the
      bitter roots
         in the month of May.
And night,
   that night,
      one night they could hear something from the west.
And they could hear 'em,
   they said,

         (*chants*) "Heeeeeee, heeeeeeee, heeeeeee … "

… four times.
And not too long,
   about twenty minutes,
      maybe half an hour, another,

         "Heeeeeeee, heeeeeee … "

… four times.
And then they kept saying that
   they could hear them.
They could hear when they fly,
   and they could hear
      it sounds like the wind.
And they watch and they listen
   because at night, you know.
And then,
   that mountain is not too far from the camp.

And then they
  flown and it stopped
    right on the point of that little peak.
And they stopped there,
  no more noise.
And then they watch 'em
  nobody sleep you know,
    they stayed awake and watched 'em.
Early in the morning,
  about two o'clock in the morning,
    maybe three o'clock in the morning.
Then they take off.
They could hear them when they started.
Awful noise, you know,
  because the winds,
    more like airplane.
And then they fly to the east.
Little ways, and they said,

      "Heeeeeeee, heeeeeeee, heeeee … "

… four times.
The next time,
  the third time,
    is quite a ways [away].
Then they don't hear 'em no more.
Not only once,
  but three times
    did they hear that on the same place.
Not on the same year,
  but maybe the year after year.
So that's why that they know
  there's supposed to be big bird
    they comes from the west.
Course I think maybe they
  floating over the world.
But they might have come up that way
  from the west
    then go that way.
So that's the stories.
All right.

They Say That Hired Man Must Be the Devil

A hired man is suddenly the subject of suspicion
when his co-workers notice that he has a tail.

All right.
This story that I'm going to tell you,
  it happens in 1905,
    down in Oregon.
And, there was a fella from North Vancouver
  by the name Mathias Joe.
He's an Indian.
He lives in North Vancouver.

And he's the one that tell me about this.

And whoever they told him, they lived there [in Oregon].
And then he heard that story about 1906 or 1905,
  is when he hear that story,
    but not all, just some—some of it.
Then Mathias Joe tell me, and then I know all about.

Down in Oregon.
And there was a ... there were rancher,
  and one man and his wife, they got no children.
They live in one place, and then their neighbour,
  they not very far from where they lived.
They could still see the house.
Could be 'bout quarter of a mile, something like that.

And this man and his wife,
  they live on a ...
    kind of uphill a little bit,
      and these others, down, a lower little.
And, there was a spring,
  from the hillside.

And there was spring water.
And this man, they tell me his name, but I didn't remember,
  anyway, there was this man and his wife,
    just the two of them.
They got no children but they got some cattle,
  and they got some horses.

So they figured they were gonna build a house.
So they build a new house,
  and then where they was on a little,
    a little mountain, not high, but just kind of round and low.
And they thought they gonna build a house right on top of that
  so it'll look nice, you know.

So they did.

But they don't know this kind of a mountain is all rock underneath.
But it is dirt on top, you know.
So they build a house.
Those days, you know, they can pipe the water on the iron pipe,
  from the spring, you know, and then it would pipe it.
And they, whoever they gonna build a house for 'em,
  they told 'em,

        "Build a house here.
          And you pipe the spring water from over there,
            and then you could put it right in the house."

So they did.
They built the house,
  and then before they started to build 'em,
    then they found out that underneath is all the rock.
So they can't put the pipe in through there.
But they set the pipe just a little ways from the house where they built.
Just the pipe there.
All they gotta do is to go out and get water.
But if it wasn't for this rock, you know,
  they could put water right inside the house, you know.

So they finished this house.
They built 'em right on a … kind of a mountain,
  just a high land.
And then they lived there for a while.

Few years after they built this house,
  and the man, they get sick.
When he sick he must have a teepee or something.
And he was sick for two, three years,
  and he go to doctor, but nothin' they can do.
Been sick for a couple of years anyway,
  then he died, the man was.

But only the woman.
And she still lived in that place,
  and they got some cattle, and horses,
    and she got lots of hay land.
And then they have to hire somebody,
  to run the ranch.
And maybe they hire someone,
  they works there not too long,
    and he quit and go away.

Finally she found a couple.
A man and his wife, and they got two children,
  one boy and one girl, they bigger one.
So she hired these people.
And these people they could stay there steady,
  the man workin' the ranch, runnin' the ranch,
    and then his boy, big boy, already about fourteen years old,
And the boy went with his dad when they work.
And the girl,
  their daughter,
    they always at the house,
      help the mother,
        and their boss, you know.

So this man, the hired man, he lived there for 'bout three, four years.
Well, just the four of 'em, you know, they run the ranch.
And this widow,
  that women that owns the place,
    is kinda, they always figured,
      she got a lot of money.

And at one time,
  while this hired man was there,
    and then there was somebody come.

Some man.
And they don't know the man.
They was a strange[r].
And they come to the house in the evening,
  just getting to be dark.
And they never seen when he come.
The first thing you know, he'd be at the door, a knock on the door.
And let him in.
They don't know where he'd come,
  and they don't know who his name was,
    and they don't know anything about 'em.
Just a strange[r].
But he come there.
But he's a nice man,
  he talks pretty good, and he's kinda lively.
And he come there a few times,
  and looks like, that hired man looks like,
    that his boss was engaged,
      might have marriage sometime,
        the way he look like.
But still they don't know the man,
  who he was and where he come from.

So they never asked him,
  they never thought to ask him.
He come a few times, but they don't know where he come.
They never see 'em, and after dark,
  Then he says,

        "Well I go. Go out."

They don't know where he go,
  and they don't know how he's come,
    either ride a horse, or walk.
They don't know.

And one time, again in the evening, and he come in.
Come back.
And they were there visiting for a while,
  then he go.
But this last time he come,
  and this hired man, they always watch him.

They was wonderin' who that man was.
They watch him this time,
 and they could see that,
   they could see it was somethin' stickin' out,
     right here, you know.
Then they watch him for a while,
 and he's got a tail.
And his tail was along his legs,
 and the end of the tail was out,
   you know, when the pants ...
     sit down and the pants like that,
       and they could see that.
And they could tell that it was a tail,
 and that it was the devil.

So they were pretty sure of that,
 so they think that's not good.
Maybe we should leave, or we should get out of here.

So he tell his wife about what he have seen.
And then he tell her,

> "We goin' to quit and then we goin' to leave.
> Right away,
>   not too long from now we go away."

And he says to his wife,

> "Don't you tell her what I see.
> Not to tell her,
>   but we can just say, 'We quit,'
>   and then we go away."

So finally this man tell his boss,

> "I think I quit,
> I've been here long enough and I'm tired of workin' here,
> I better quit."

So this woman says,

> "No, you should not quit.
> You get used to it.
> You been here long enough,

and you know all the work.
You should not quit.
Maybe I should raise your wages a little more.
I want you to stay."

"No," he said, "I want to quit, I want to go away,
    go someplace and work."

So finally they go away.

But this woman was all alone, again,
  and they hire somebody,
    but they stay just a few days, not too long,
      and they go.

About another couple of years, or one year anyway.
And their neighbour is not far.
They could still see the house, you know,
    like 'bout a quarter of a mile or something like that.
And there was a road, something like this road.
And the road goes by this other people's house,
  like from here to those trees over there.
Could be 'bout a hundred yards or more.
That was the road goin' by.

And one evening,
  about four o'clock in the afternoon, four or five,
    this man that lived there, he got a son.
His son was about fourteen years old.
And they were in the house when they see somebody goin' by on
  horseback,
    ridin' a roan horse.
Strawberry roan, the horse was.
Good lookin' horse.
And they got new saddle.
They could see because the new saddle it's red,
  like in fifty yards or a hundred yards
    they could tell that they got a new saddle.
But they see 'em go by.
And they got nice clothes, all new, good clothes,
  wears good clothes, and good saddle, good horse.

And he go by.

They watch him.
And they go up a little bit,
  and they come to that woman's place.
They could see him from the house.
And he stopped, and he walked to the house.
After a while they come out, the woman come out.
The both of 'em went into a shed, you know,
  where they got the tools and stuff.
And then they were over there,
  and looks like they unsaddled the horse,
    and hanged the saddle in the shed.
And then they could watch.
Not too far, maybe like from here to the edge these bushes,
  maybe a little more.
So they went out in the field.
And it's getting to be 'bout, could be around five-thirty
  somethin' like that.
Then they went out in the field,
  and they could see them hammerin' the post, you know,
    they hammer, and hammer.
Then the rope there and they tie his horse
  so he could feed there for overnight.
And then they went back to the house,
  and they don't see them there, but they see the horse there,
    'til it gets dark.

And next mornin',
  they looked that way, but the horse was not there.

Nothin'.

So they leave it that way all day.
Nobody 'round.

Then, getting to be evenin' the next day.
Then they tell this man tell his son,

        "You better go over there and check up.
          Maybe you check the saddle, her saddle, if it's there."

They got three horses,
  that woman.

The other two, that's a team of horses,
   but one of 'em just a saddle horse.

So this man think maybe early that morning,
   and they might take her horse
      and they might both ride and go someplace.

If they miss the horse and the saddle belongs to the woman—
   well, they might go away.

So he sent the boy over there.

And the boy went and looked at the place,
   and the saddle is there, that woman's saddle,
      but they don't see no other saddle.
And then they go out in the field, and they see the horses,
   they were still there, the three of them.

But the woman, there don't seems to be nobody at the house.

So he comes back and then he says,

      "I don't see nothin' but the saddle is there,
         and then the horses were there.
            And this horse is been stick there, that strawberry roan."

The boy went over there and he don't seems to see any tracks,
   or anything like that.
They tell his dad, but it's gettin' late.

The next morning, him and his dad they went over there.
And the old man, they looked around where they stick the horse,
   because they watch 'em.

When they get there,
   no tracks,
      no horse manure,
         no sticks there,
            nothin'.
Supposedly if the horse sticks there, then they could eat the grass,
   then they could see the tracks.

But there is nothin'.

So they went to the house.
Then they knocked on the door.

No answer.
Nobody in there seems to be.

Him and his son,
  but they stood there awhile,
    and they could hear somethin'.

Sounds like some kind of a music, or somethin'.
Sounds like in the house.
And then they opened the door.
They not locked.
They open.
And they come in,
  in the house like this,
    in the sitting room.
But it was a bedroom,
  that got a door.
So they walked over there,
  but they don't open.
They stood and listened.
And then they could hear somethin' in there when they get close.
And it sounds like a snake.

So they leave it.
Never open 'em
  and they go back.

And then the man, they think,

> "I better report this.
>   It don't sounds very good what I hear,
>   what we hear in the bedroom."

So they go to town and they report this to the policeman.

And then a bunch of 'em come,
  the policeman and some other ones.

And they all get there,

and then the policeman comes,
and they all go in and stood and listen.

"It sounds like a snake is in there."

Then of course the policeman,
they got to open 'em,
and they try the door and it's not locked.

And they open.

And they looked in there,
and then supposing if this was the room,
and the bed is on that side,
and the door open that way,
you still couldn't see the bed right away,
but on this side.

Soon as they open 'em, and they see a snake.
They stood.
Snake is about this big.
And they stood up,
they put their tail in like that in the floor.
And then they stood up 'bout this high,
a bunch of 'em, 'bout six or seven,
along the bed, and they all rattlin'.

And finally they open the door a little more to look to the bed,
and they see the woman were layin' the bed,
still her eyes were open, and was not asleep.
And the great big snake were laying alongside of her,
the big one.
Then they were long,
and their tail, it coiled in the foot, like.
And their head—
they were together and lay on the bed.
And the other ones they all stood,
and they all rattle.

Then the policeman says,

"You guys come and see."

And they all went over there, one at a time,
  take a look, come back, and then the other one.

So that's what they see and then they close the door,
  and they went out.

Then they went and reported again,
  and figured out what they should do.

Finally, they thought maybe they should burn the house.
They just burn 'em, just like the way they are,
  and just start the fire,
    the next day.

So a lot of man come.
And then they put oil,
  coal oil around the house,
    and then they put it onto the house.
And they still hear them,
  they still there.

And then they start the fire.
They burned the house.
And then they went away.
And then they watched the house still on the fire.
All at once they start the fire clean around,
  and the fire start all at once.
And they watch from the distance,
  they don't see anythin' goin' out.
The door is not locked.

Nothin' goin' out.

The house was burnt.

And they watch 'em 'til the house all burn,
  and it's hot, you know,
    and they don't see anything.
Leave 'em there 'til he gets cooled off in a couple days.
And they went over there,
  and they could never see no other bone but the woman's bone,
    in the bed.
They were there,

they must have been layin' in the bed,
  'til they were burnt,
    and the bed was just smashed down like by fire,
      and her bone it still there.

But no other one.

No other bone.
Just snakes.
They should have a bone,
  But they not there.

So they leave 'em there for a while,
  and they tell 'em they could clean them.
Everything, clean 'em and haul 'em away,
    and dump 'em someplace.
A long ways off.

And they do that.
They clean 'em and everythin'.
They clean up and they take that bone
  and bury 'em.
And they clean everythin'.

When the house was burnt,
  they could see all the rock underneath.
But this rock was kind of a crack in some places.
They're 'bout this big, this wide.
There's a lot of these cracks.

So in a year or so after that,
  then they could see there was a lot of snakes right in that place.
The little snake, you know,
  but a lot of 'em.
So they make a den in that place.
In those rocks there that got a crack.
And that's where the snakes, they make a den there,
  and there are lots of 'em.
But they don't see no big snake,
  but just the little ones, but lots of 'em.

And then the sheep man come in.

And he make a camp at the spring,
  the spring is not too far from that place where they burned the house.

And they told him,

      "There's a lot of snakes there.
       You should not put in a camp there."

But he says,

      "Ah, that don't matter. I put camp here."

So he put camp at the spring.

Not too long,
  when he were out herdin' sheep,
   and then he come back
    and there's a lot of snakes there,
     at his camp.
And the scrap bacon and any kind of a grub,
  and the snakes they eat that.

So the sheepman, he's just gotta scram outta there,
  because they couldn't stay there.
First he put in the camp, the snake never was there,
  they don't go,
   but they all right for a few days.

But the snakes,
  they went over there.
When he come back one day and there's all kinds of snakes at this camp.
And they just had to beat it.

So they know the snakes that they come out from there,
  they make a den there.
So they figure out what they're goin' to do 'bout it.

And then it was winter time.
It comes to be winter.

And the snake go in the den.
And they know it's in there.

So they figure out they goin' to get the dynamite,
  the black powder.

Then they get lots of them,
  and they fill up,
    they clean the snow,
      and they clean everything so it's springtime.
Then they fill up all these cracks with the dynamite.
They fill 'em up, all the cracks.
And then they got wire like this and then they got a big battery way out.
And they put the wires on the battery,
  and they switch it.

And all at once (*clap*)—
  they have explosion.
And this rock it don't blow out,
  it just smash everything.

And they leave 'em that way for a while,
  and they look,
    all the scraps that they clean up,
      they just kinda smashed.

No more snakes.

They kill 'em all.
And they all right.

So this Mathias, Joe Mathias,
  he worked for that man.
And this man who they seen there—
  that's the older man,
    and he died.

But there was the son that was fourteen years old,
  he's the one, him and his dad,
    they seen it first place.
And he's the one that told him.
He's still at the house,
  but his dad died.
But that's not told.
But he's getting to be 'bout, somewhere 'round,
Getting to be 'bout eighteen or twenty years old then.
And he looks after the ranch.
And that Mathias is workin' for him there.
And they don't tell him right away

but he was workin' there for quite a while,
  two, three months.
Then they tell him,
  and they take him over there,
    and they showed him where they burned the house,
      and the explosion in this place and all that.

So we heard that kind of a story,
  but not all.
They just say the woman was found in her house,
  there was some snake in there,
    with 'em.
That's all we heard about.
But Mathias, they tell me all about what happened.

  Wendy: That's quite a story!

It's not very good but it happens that way.

So the first place that hired man—
  they say that man that comes,
    that must be the devil.
Because he's got the tail along his leg
  and they could see the end of the tail here.
And that's the same one,
  could be the same one that rides on that roan horse,
    and stop there.
And that's the same one that turns into a snake then.

Not very good (*laughs*).
But that's true.
Not too long ago,
  that happened in 1905.

So nowadays,
  nobody know.
They seems to forget 'em.

But I still remember that story.
So that's the end of it.

THEY CONFESSED ALL ABOUT WHAT THE CAT TOLD HIM

A man has an unusual encounter with a cat.

Story number three
  is still cat story.
So this is the number three,
  the cat speak to the man.
And this man ...
  his name, Sammy.
That's all I know,
  his last name
    I couldn't remember
      but his first name was Sammy.
He used to live in,
  they call it Kartar Valley
    that's in the other end of Omak Lake
      about three, four miles from the end of the lake
      in that Kartar Valley.
That's where that Sammy lives.
And he's quite a drinker,
  he drinks
    lots.
And he's got a house,
  and he's got a wife,
    and he got two, three children.
But still, he's,
  he's an awful drinker.
And then he's kind of mean
  with his people,
    with his wife,
      with his kids.
And because his wife would tell him,

      "Should not drink too much."

Then he get mad.
They want to drink.
And they got some,
   they got quite a bit of property, you know,
      they got some cattle, and the horses, and ...
But they want to sell 'em.
They want to sell them to ...
   so they can get money
      and then drink.
They did.
Finally, they went broke.
They sell all the things they got—
   cattle, and the stuff, you know ...
But still own the land and the house.
And his wife got mad,
   and then they left 'em
      and the wife go away.
Take the kids along with 'em.
But only himself at the house.
But he's got no,
   no stock no more,
      they went broke.
But they get money,
   they sell the cattle and
      land, they sell the land
         and they got money.
So they take off and went away.
They went in the States,
   way down California
      and down that way ...
They just go.
And the first thing you know,
   they was way down in Texas.
And they went broke.
They got no money.
So he figures he's going to come home
   from Texas.
But he's got no money.
They can't take the train,
   they can't take the bus,
      nothing because ...

They can only walk.
Anyhow, they hike from Texas.
And they walk, you know,
  they kept a-coming.
No money.
No nothing.
They get hungry.

And then they come by to some house,
  some ranchers ...
And they went over there, and ask for job,
  see if they can get a job.
They might get a job, and get paid,
  so they'll have a little money.
No, they wouldn't give 'em jobs.
So they ask for job every place where they come to,
  they could never get a job.
In one place, they come.
Come up the road and they
  see a man with a pail, you know,
    walking towards the pig pen.
And they feeding the pig[s],
  there're two cans of potatoes boiled,
    and some kind of meat with 'em.
To feed the pigs.
And they're watching that,
  it looks like they could see the pig pen, you know.
And then this man,
  the one carrying the pails.
And he think
  that man, maybe he's going to feed the pigs.
    I better wait 'til he feed the pigs;
      when they go back
        then I can go over there and eat some of that.

Because he's hungry.

So they wait there awhile.
And this man,
  they come to feed to the pigs, you know
    and then go back.
So after he go back,

and they went over there
  and they get some of that
    they get potatoes, and there was some ...
      horse meat or something, you know,
        kind of bad meat
          but it's all right for the pig.
And then he eat that,
  because they can eat that,
    he's hungry.
So this man, he feed the pigs
  and then he look
    he see that man go to the pig pen.
He was wondering why,
  and then he watch 'em.
And they went in the ...
  get behind something so they wouldn't see 'em, you know.
But they watch 'em.
They watch 'em awhile there,
  and they could tell they was eating from the pigs' feed.
So they go over there.
And they get there
  and this man, Sammy,
    they was still eating potatoes and meat from the pig.
And they told him,

> "You better quit that.
>   You can come
>   and I can give you something to eat.
>   You must have been hungry to do that.
>   Leave that alone,
>   that's not good,
>   that's only for the pig."

All right.
He went with that man.
And this man, he's got his own cabin,
  and they got some grub there.
But he's working for the ranch, you know.
So when they get in there,
  and then they give 'em something to eat there.
And he eat that 'til he get enough, and they ...
  they told this man,

       "You can give me lunch.
         Then I'll go."

So this man, they give 'em big lunch.
And he went.
They go a long ways, walking.
And they eat that lunch of his, and then they
  finish 'em.
No more.
Then they still, still walking.
And they get hungry again.
And they was wondering where they can get
  another lunch, or
    where they can get to eat ...
Nothing.
No place—
  nobody want them.
They kept going, and they go by
  some house, maybe
    kind of farm, you know.
And then they go by there, and they
  turn off and then they
    ask for job.

       "No, we got no job."

So they kind of mad,
  and then they turn around and go.
But he didn't know
  the cat was followed him.
He did not know
  'til he get quite a ways out.
Towards evening,
  getting to be in the afternoon.

And he was walking along,
  then he heard the cat behind him,
    the cat was right behind him.
The cat,

      "Meow! Meow!"

You know, they look back.

And the cat was right behind him,
  right on his heels.
So they get a stone,
  and throw the stone,
    they chase 'em away.
Then they kept going.
Not too long,
  then he heard that cat,

  "Meow! Meow!"

Looked.
That was the same cat.
He was behind him,
  pretty close.
And they get mad.
They looked around,
  they picked up a stone,
    they throw the stone at 'em,
      and the cat running,
        they told 'em,

  "Go away."

There he go.
Not too long,
  he heard that,
    the same

  "Meow! Meow!"

Looked,
  that was the same cat.
And he's going to do that again.
But the cat told 'em,

  "Leave me alone,
   let me tell you something."

… in their language.

So they
  kind of surprised, you know,
    the cat talked to 'em.

So they stop
  and the cat told 'em,

        "You should not do that.
        I'm going to
          treat you good.
        I want to do some good for you.
        But you want to do bad for me.
        You chasing me with the stick and stone.
        But I ...
          I still figure I'm going to
            treat you good.
        But you've got to do what I say."

The cat told him.

So I guess he must have said "all right."
Of course, they must have (*laughs*).
So the cat told him,

        "Now, instead of chasing me with a stick or stone,
            you pick me up and then you
              put me in your arm and you
                hold me.
        Then you walk on the road.
        And not too long,
          not too far from here
            and there was a forks of the road.
        One road that way
          and the other road
            that way.
        You can come to that
          that forks of the road
            and you look
              just where the road turns off that way,
              and the other one that way.
        Right in the middle, there.
        Then you could lay me down,
          [on] my back.
        And then you could take your jackknife,
          and then you could cut my breast here,
            cut it open.

205

Don't you think—
　　I'll be alive,
　　　　but you cut me anyway.
Then I'll be dead after you cut.
And then you can cut my heart out.
And you take my heart,
　　and then you got a handkerchief,
　　　　you roll 'em in your handkerchief
　　　　and put it in your pocket.
And then you can go to the left road.
This is the right road,
　　right side of the road,
　　　　as they going that way,
　　　　　right side of the road,
　　　　　　and the left side of the road."

And the cat told him,

　　"When you leave me
　　　after you take my heart,
　　　　then you take me way off the road
　　　　　out of the sight,
　　　　　　so nobody could see me laid there
　　　　　　　and then you could laid me there,
　　　　　　　　put me there, and I'd be laid there.
And then you can go back to the same place.
But you take the left road.
And then you walk on the left road for a ways,
　　maybe could be around twenty minutes,
　　　may be half-hour ...
　　　　you might know something."

All right.
They pick up the cat
　and then they hold him on his arm,
　　walking down the road.
And it's getting to be evening,
　getting to be late, like,
　　could be around
　　　four or five o'clock in the evening.
They're not too far,

and they see that forks in the road.
And they come to the place
  and then look,
    this is the centre.
The road that way,
  and the road that way.
So they put the cat down.
And they get his knife,
  and then the cat, they lay down on the back.
And they cut 'em open.
And they cut,
  they just chopped,
    and they dead.
And they cut this,
  and they cut 'em open, and they
    feel around to find his little heart, you know,
      just small.
Then they get that,
  and the blood, you know,
    they wipe the blood out.
Get his handkerchief and roll 'em in his handkerchief
  and then they put 'em in his pocket.
And then they take this cat
  and they take him way off the road
    out of the sight
      and they laid him there
        and then they talked to him, he says,

          "I put you here,
            now you're going to be here [for] all time."

Then they go back,
  the same place and then they
    go to the left road.
And then it's getting to be pretty near dark.
And they kept walking for a ways ...
The first thing you know—
  they got a coat on, you know,
    just like my coat here—
      and they could feel,
        this coat was getting tight.

Getting tighter.
What's the matter?
My coat is tight.
And he put his hands in the pocket,
  and it's full of stuff in each pocket
    and then they pull out ...
They all money.
Full of money on each pocket.
Not only on the coat,
  but on his pants pocket, and
    shirt pocket, and
      every pocket.
All money.
Ten-dollar bill,
  fifty-dollar bill,
    hundred-dollar bill ...
By God, he pulled them all out, and then
  by God, he got a lot of money.
So that's the cat—
  they give him that money.
So they kept walking 'til they come to a town.
So they looked around,
  and they see the cafe,
    and they go in there and eat
      and then they go out and they look around,
        they see the rooming house,
          and then they buy a room and then
            they sleep in there.
Next day they went to the station,
  and they took the train
    and then they come home on the train.
Because he's got a lot of money.
And then they got back home.
And then he was home.
Still they got a lot of money.
But when he get home,
  not too long,
    then his memory seems to be turning.
Not so good.
And some of the people,

the Indian people there
  told him,

          "What's the matter, you?
            Your memory don't seems to be right."

So, they never said nothing.
But two, three times he was asked.
And then he said,

          "I know it's not good, my memory."

And they tell him,

          "You must be doing something.
            What you did?"

So finally, they confessed, you know.
They tell all about
  what the cat told 'em, and
    what they did with cat and
      all that.
So these people,
  they told the priest.
And the priest said,

          "You tell him to come,
            I want to see 'em."

So somebody told him,

          "The priest want to see you."

They went
  and see the priest.
And the priest asked 'em,

          "What [did] you do?
            You did this, you did that?"

          "Yeah, I did that."

          "And where's the money?
            Do you still got the money?"

"Oh yes,
         I still got 'em."

The priest says,

         "Let me see."

And then they pull out his pocket,
   and they show that to the priest.
The priest looked at the money,
   and he says,

         "This is money,
            but it's not real money.
         But I'll bless [it] for you,
            and then it become to be
               real money."

         "All right, you do that."

So they begin to believe
   in Catholic way then.

So the priest,
   they blessed that money,
      and give 'em back,
         but still they ...
            their memory turnin' all the time.

Pretty soon they go crazy.
So they,
   finally they have to take him to the crazy house.
And he stay in the crazy house,
   they never get better
      and then he die.
Sammy, that's what they do with the cat, you know.
But they didn't last long—
   they got home, all right—
      but they died.
That's the end of that stories.

Shut it off for a minute.

THESE CATTLE, THEY COME OUT FROM THE LAKE

Palmer Lake is the site of some strange occurrences.

The next, that's the same place in Palmer Lake.
There was an Indian
  on this end of that lake.
You seen that lake,
  we go by there.
Did you?
When we go to Omak, we go through Nighthawk.
And then we keep going that way.
We go through Loomis.
Remember that?

   Wendy: Yeah.

That's Palmer Lake,
  on this end.
That's where the Indian was.
It's in this end of the lake.
And then to the west,
  close to the mountain,
    and there was a brushy land
    and there was a spring water.
And that's where the Indians camp.
I don't know what they getting,
  but I think they just go up the hill and hunt.
And that's why they campin' there.

And, one night there was a moonlight night.
And one night when they all stop and they just about—
  some of them go to bed already,
    but some of 'em didn't—
    and they heard some cattle.

They were bawling
  along the shore.
That's not too far from where they are.
They heard the cattle were bawling.
Sounds like the bull been fightin'
  and they could hear the bull was bawling.
So they know,
  there is no cattle in that area.
There was some cattle,
  but it's way this way.
But they thought,
    maybe these cattle they might go that far
    and then they got a fight or something.
So they listen to that for quite a while
  and then they heard 'em bawlin'
    and it looks like the bull was fightin',
      sounds like.
And it seems to go to the east, like,
  that way.
But they all sand, you know,
  they all sand, soft ground along the shore.
This end.
So, in the morning, the next morning,
  they thought maybe they should see the tracks
    and find out which way,
      where did these cattle come from?
They know there was some cattle,
  a lot of cattle,
    but it's way this way.
They figure they shouldn't be over there.
They was wondering where these cattle come from.

Anyway they went over there
  and then they could see the tracks.
All the tracks just look like they coming out from the lake.
Then they get on the dry land.
Then they kind of travel that way,
  move towards the east
    and then they must've been fighting.
They could see the tracks, you know,
  where they fight, you know.

Then they make the ground—stir it up.
And then they go that way
  and they fight around a little ways,
    about a quarter of a mile or more.
And all the tracks in the lake seems to go in the lake.
And look for some more,
  no other tracks, nowhere.
That same track come out,
  and then the same track, that's all.

So they know these cattle,
  that they come out from the lake.
And they go into the lake
  but they don't see 'em.
But they heard them and they see the tracks.
That's all.
Shut off.
That's just a short stories.

> *Harry paused for just a few minutes before adding the following segment.*

But, I remember one time you ask me
  for that cow which went across the lake.
Palmer Lake.
And the lake was wide.
Could be about a mile wide.
But that is supposed to be the narrowest spot
  like in that lake.
The rest of 'em is wider.
Or maybe not a mile,
  but it's quite a ways.
Could be three-quarter of a mile anyway.
And, the two, three man,
  they were driving cattle from the mountain.
And they drive 'em down.
Then they was trying to cut off the bunch, you know,
  they drive 'em in different place.
But the one cow, they got wild like.
They chase 'em around too much
  and then they got kind of mad, I guess.

But they try to head 'em off.
They want to go to the other bunch
  but they chase 'em 'til they jumped in the water.
So they stop and they watch 'em.
They swim right across.
Where that about three-quarter of a mile wide.
And they watch 'em,
  they thought they not going to make it.
But finally they get on the other side.
And whoever, they tell me that,
  he is the one they chase 'em around
    and some others.
They two, three cowboys.
And that's his cow, too.
And that's something, you know,
  I seen that place
    and don't look like any animal can swim across.
But that cow, they made it.
That's right in Palmer Lake.
That's all.

The Cat Told Him, "You Not Going to Last Long!"

A cat teaches an important lesson.

The cat changed himself into a ...
   into a big cat,
     about four times as big as he was
     at one time.

Remember when we [were] driving
  and you see that little cabin on top of the little mountain?
That was the place.

And this lady
 I know her,
   she used to work for us—
    they used to stay with us,
     do the cooking for us,
      when we were on the ranch.
And this lady,
 she *hate* the cat.
They don't like cat.
I don't know why.

We always have a cat,
  I and the wife, you know,
  we had a cat,
   maybe one or two,
   all the time.

And then she stays with us,
  do the cooking,
   working for us.
And she know that we love the cat
 we like cat[s] and we
  treat 'em good.

She don't like that.
They don't say nothing.
But I can tell, you know—
  we can tell by the looks.

And then when they think
    that we didn't watch 'em
      then they could kick the cat—
        kick 'em, you know.
Or they can open the door
  and then if she think that we didn't watch 'em
    then they kick 'em
      and get the broom and
        let 'em out.
They don't like it,
  they don't like cat[s].
And we treat the cat good
  and then we feed 'em,
    and I take some of the saucer, you know,
      and I put milk in there
        and I laid 'em on the floor
          and they lick that.
God, she don't like that.

And I watch 'em,
  and sometimes she pick up that saucer
    and they clean, and they clean 'em good
      because the cat they eat in there,
        they don't like that.
And then I take the certain one
  and she could never use that saucer.
They could put it for me,
  or for her, you know, for my wife,
    but she never could use
      because the cat
        they eat that.

See how much,
  you know, how much they don't like the cat?
So they was like that at all time.

And that time,
　　that was her cabin,
　　　that little mountain you seen
　　　　and you said that little mountain that's on top
　　　　and I says,

　　　　"There was a stories about [that]."

So that was the place,
　　that was her house.

And they got a husband,
　　and they got a brother.
And her brother was staying with them.
And this man,
　　they work on hay.
There was,
　　across the road,
　　　I told you that was hay land [at] one time.
But now it is orchard.
And that,
　　whoever own that hay, and
　　　these mans, so they go over there
　　　　and work.
They cut the hay,
　　and they
　　　take 'em away, you know,
　　　　they stack 'em,
　　　　　they working on that hay.
But they go back to the house
　　and they board there.
And then she does the cooking for them,
　　for the boys.

And one day
　　the cat, these wild cats, you know,
　　　there was a lot of people around there,
　　　　they got some cat[s] and then
　　　　　they run out, you know,
　　　　　　they went away.

And once in a while,
   the cat maybe one or two,
      maybe three cat[s]
         then they come 'round the house.
And those days, you know ...
   now today that you got a can or something,
      anything waste you put 'em in there
         and then you take 'em away,
            to dump 'em.
But those days, you know,
   anything, they just throw 'em outside.
And then the cat come
   and they eat that.
And still she don't like to see the cat eat around there
   what she throw.
And then they see the cat
   eat that and they get the stone
      and hit 'em with the stone.
They throw the stone at 'em,
   the cat run away ...
They don't like 'em.
And they get the stick
   and then they throw the stick at the cat ...
And one day they do that again,
   when the boys were out working.
Before noon.
The boys go to work, you know,
   but she's still at the house.
And they go out and they see the cat ...
One cat was spotted cat,
   kinda pinto cat.
They was mad.

They look around,
   get a stick,
      and then they throw the stick at the cat,
         and then
            they look around for some more,
               they want to find [a] stone.
And then they look
   and they see the cat was about so high.

That spotted cat.
You know, the cat was just about this high.
Little, but when they seen 'em,
  they was about this big,
    about four times as big as they was.

And by God,
  she was scared.
And the cat was looking at her.
And they stopped
  from throwing the rocks at 'em.
And the cat told 'em,

> "That was all right.
>   You don't like me.
>   But you['re] not going to last
>   from now on.
>   I can be last,
>   but you['re] not going to last."

That's what the cat told her.
She says, but I don't know.
Maybe they just hear that, or
    maybe the cat is not so big, maybe
      just only on her eyes.
Never know.
But that's what she says.
And then
  they looked at it for a while there,
    and the cat was pretty big and then
      their hair was all standing up.
And their eyes was big and yellow ...
  and they talked to her.
And that's what they tell 'em,

> "You['re] not going to last long."

So ...
  they look in the second
    for something.
And then they could see that cat was
  just the same, you know

the ordinary cat,
  and then they run.

But they could feel
  all her body was just ...
    just like itchy, or something, you know—
    all over.
And their memory seems to be turning.
And then they go back in the house,
  and lay down,
    but still is not good.
And she's supposed to cook, you know,
  about eleven o'clock,
    and then they could do the cooking
      when the boys come in for dinner.
But they didn't cook.
They not good.
So the boys come back for dinner,
  and then they come to the house—
    no fire, no cook—
      but they was there, but
        nothing.
So they come in and
  ask 'em,

      "What's the matter?"

They lay on the bed.
So they get up and they
  talk, but they can tell they['re] not good.
Seems to be like
  paralyzed or something.
And they ask 'em,

      "What's the matter, you?
       What's wrong with you?"

And then they tell all what,
  what she done, and what she seen
    what the cat told 'em.
They mention that, all.
And then ...

they don't look good,
  and they kind of shaky.
So they take 'em to hospital,
  take 'em to doctor,
    to Tonasket.
But what doctor can do about that?
He don't know what's wrong.
And they kept 'em there for a while, and
  not two days after that
    they dead.
Because the cat told 'em,

      "You not going to last long."

And then it was.
She didn't last long.
Just from doing that,
  just for hate the cat.
See, that's only short stories,
  that's the end of that story.

THE CALF, THEY GOT NO EYES

A blind calf disappears.

And this is a stories, that's still in Omak Lake.
But in the other end,
  in the south end.
That's not long time ago.
That's could be 'round,
  oh, around seventy, eighty years ago.
And, there was some Indians living in that end of the lake.
On the south end of the lake.
A little ways from there.
About two, three miles from the end of the lake.
And some Indians, they got a place there.
They got a ranch.
And one of these Indians,
  they got a lot of cattle in there.
And his cattle was—
They run all over the place
  and at the end of that lake
    and on the hillside.
His cattle was all over.
So, like every day him and his wife,
  they go out on horseback and look around
    and look at the cattle.
And sometimes they find the newborn calf, you know.
And then they find that,
  if it was young cow they had a calf,
    not enough milk.
And then they take 'em.
And mother and all.
And they take 'em and take 'em to the ranch
  and take care of 'em, you know.
Because the mother not much milk.

Only young.
But sometimes they found the cow they had the calf,
  well that's an only cow,
    well they all right.
They just let 'em go.
They watch that, you know.
If there's any of these cows not enough milk,
  they take 'em to the place
    and they got some milk cows there
      and then they feed the calves.
They take care of 'em so they wouldn't lose 'em.
That's what they doing every day when they goes out.

One day they were out,
  looked around, and they found a calf.
This calf is not just born,
  it seems to be older.
They must've been born, could be around ten days or more.
Kind of older, but they found him all alone.
So they wait there.
They thought maybe the mom come back.
And then they could see him,
  that this calf, they got no eyes.
No nothing.
No eyes.
They just got no eyes.
They all, just all like that.
No eyes.
But it is bigger.
So, there was one of them,
  they thought maybe they were here all the time.

          "Maybe the mom, they goes out and they must've come back,
            and give him the milk, and suck, you know,
              and go back.
          We could wait and we could know which one was his mom.
          And then we could take him too—
            he was a bull calf.
          We could take him to the ranch and raise him.
          Doesn't matter if they can't see.
          When he get big, we can butcher him."

That's what they thought.
So, they got no rope.
And the man, he take his shirt off.
And I think the lady, they used to have,
  those days, you know, the womens, they have the skirt.
And they took that out, the top one,
  and they twist that
    and tie 'em together.
And then they tie the calf in the neck.
And tie 'em onto the sagebrush,
  the strong sagebrush,
    it's different sagebrush over there.
So they thought they going to be tied,
  otherwise they might go.
When they come back,
    they going to lost 'em.
And they's too big to carry.
So they go back to the house, to the place,
  and they going to bring the buggy.
Single-horse buggy.
And they going to bring that buggy as far as they can get them.
And then they going to take this calf
  and make 'em walk.
They could steer 'em, you know,
  because they can't see.
'Til they get them to buggy.
And then they could load 'em on the buggy
  and tie their legs
    and take 'em home.
That's what they figures.

So they tie 'em there in case they might go away
  and then they couldn't find 'em
    because it's sagebrush.
And while they were away, quite a ways,
  it take 'em about an hour and a half or so,
    then they come back.
And where they tie 'em,
  they must've pulled back and broke that cloth, you know,
    and still they had some on the neck.
The part of it, but the other part,

they broke.
And then they went.
They could see his track.
And they follow his track
  and they keep going,
    turn that way,
      and that way,
        that way.
They go straight to the lake.
They follow the tracks,
  and they follow them,
    until they come to the edge of the lake
      and then they walked in the water
        and they all sand in the water,
          all this sand.
They could see his track
  and then they follow the track 'til it gets too deep.
And his tracks still head that way
  and then no more.

And looks like they must've come out from the water.
And lay around.
And then they go back
  and they get in the water.
They don't see them no more.
But they got no eyes.
That's another funny thing.

Shut her off.

The Big Fish Swallow That Horse

*A missing horse mysteriously turns up
on the side of Palmer Lake.*

Indians were camped on the east side of Palmer Lake.
They camp there in time to get there—
  because they pickin' some saskatoon.
So they camp along the shore there,
  at Palmer Lake.
A bunch of Indian.
Not only one or two,
  but a bunch of 'em.
Some of them, they pickin' saskatoon,
  and some of 'em they hunt for deer
    and groundhog and things like that.
And one old man, he got a nice horse.
Not very big, this horse.
It's just small,
  but it's a big horse.
Gentle, and young horse.
It'd be about five, six years old
  and it's pretty gentle.
Good horse.
And he always ride that horse to hunt.

And then, they rode that horse
  and then they hunt one day, and then they come back at the camp
  in the evening.
And they all come back
  because they—
    a lot of them out hunting
      and some of 'em,
        they wanted to stay,

went out to pick saskatoon
        and at night they all come back to the camp.
So, this man, his name is Show-MUH
That means, Show-MUH, it means,
  "off the road."
Could be "standing off the road."
That's his Indian name.
So he come home,
  come back to the camp.
And then the rest of them did,
  they all come back.
And then they turn his horse loose.
They turn 'em loose.
Because these others, they own horses too.
And when they come back,
  And then they unsaddle the horses
    and turn 'em loose.
So Show-MUH turn his horse loose.

The next morning, they had to go out
  and get their horses
    and then they can go out hunting.
And Show-MUH they went,
  all of 'em went
    and they get the horses.
But his horse is not in the bunch.
He don't know what happened,
  where they go.
They should be in the bunch of the same ones—
  there are a lot of horses.
But his horse is not in the bunch.
So they have to look for that horse.
And maybe some of the boys,
  they hunt and lookin' for that horse.
They couldn't find 'em.
They look for that horse all day.
There is nowhere to go.
The place is not very big.
He should be around.
But they could never find 'em.

They look for that horse all day,
  couldn't find 'em,
    next day,
      three, four days,
        look for that horse
        and never did find.
They never see no tracks,
  and no sign or nothing.
They don't know what happened to that horse.

So they thought maybe someone,
  maybe some Indian from someplace,
    they might come at night and stole that horse.
Take 'em somewhere.
Only ways they could figure out.
So, every year, they always had the camp in that place,
  every year.
So they forget this horse
  because they couldn't find 'em.
They have to wait long time.
Next year.
And the Indians go to same place
  and they had the camp there.
And Show-MUH was in the bunch.
And one day the boys, the little boys, you know,
  just kids,
    and they running 'round along the shore
      and then they taking a bath, you know,
        in the lake
         and running around.
So finally they come to one place
  and then they seen a horse.
It lays right at the edge of the water.
Lays there, the part of it,
  lays in the water.
But the part of it,
  just in the edge of the water
    where the horse was laying.
These boys, what they seen.

The little boys.
They looks like fresh.

So they run to the camp
  and they said to the other Indians,

> "We found a horse,
>   laying right in the edge of the lake.
> He dead.
> But they lay there.
> Their nose was bleedin'."

So, the other Indians say,

> "You boys are liars.
>   There's nothing there."

> "Yeah," he says.
> "We seen 'em."

So finally they went over there.
And they see that horse.
And that's Show-MUH's horse, that's the one they missed a year.
One year ago.
And they tell him.
He's an old man, you know.
They tell him,

> "Your horse was found over there.
>   They lay there dead though."

So they went over there
  and see that horse,
    if that was his horse.
If that was the one they missed,
  a year ago in that area.
But he was lay there,
  just fresh.
So fresh, and his nose was bleeding.
He just die.
And they don't know how come to be like that.

Where did he come from there to be lay there?
But anyway, they fresh.

So they thought,

   "We might as well skin 'em
    and eat 'em
     because they're fat
      and they just die."

It's good eating,
 because those days they eat the horse.
They skin 'em and eat 'em.

Anyhow, they skin 'em
 because they fresh.
Skin 'em and cut 'em.
And they had a good roast
 and then they dry 'em
 and then they eat 'em.
In about the first night,
 the second night,
  and one Indian doctor,
   not Show-MUH,
    but this is another one,
     they sleep
      and they could see in his dream.
There was something happen.
Then he sing his song all night.
Then, in the morning, the other people tell 'em,

   "What's wrong with you?
    You might've be see something last night.
    You sing all night."

He said,

   "Yeah, I did.
   I did find out something.
   That horse, last year, Show-MUH's horse,
    they turn 'em loose.
   And that horse, they walked little ways.
   Not too far.

Get out of the sight.
They think they can go over there and drink.
They went to the water and drink.
There was something coming out of the water.
And they swallow, the big fish or—
   whatever it is, they were big one.
They swallow that horse.
Then it went in the water
   and it kept them in there all winter.
Still inside of that,
   whatever it is."

They call 'em *ha-HEET*.
That's supposed to monster in the water.
But it's supposed to be big.
And, they kept 'em there one year.
Then they come back.
They put them there so the people can see.
Then it's not this horse,
  they never die.
They still alive.
But when they put them there,
  they leave 'em there
   and then left 'em
    and then the horse die.
That's why the people see they just fresh.
They just dead when the boys found 'em.
But it's inside of something in the water,
  still alive.

That's all.
That's the end of that story.

THAT CAT WAS TRYING TO HELP HIM FROM GOING TO HELL

A spotted cat tries to help Tom Daley.

This stories
  it was a cat stories, all right but ...
    it's not bad,
      or anything.
There was a fella lives in
  the other side of Keremeos,
    about three miles.
They call it Daley Bluff.
And his name, Daley,
  Tom Daley.
That's how come they call that bluff Daley Bluff.
He's got a ranch there,
  they big ranch.
Got lots of hay, and
  lots of cattle.
And they got some children
  some of the children they're big, you know,
    big boy.
And they got some hired mans,
  that do the haying.
They got a lot of hay.
And my dad and another three Indians,
  four of them,
    all Indian
      they work for him.
And two of these other Indians
  one of them he runs the ...
    they cutting hay, you know,
      on horse mower.
And the other one there, they rake—
  they rake the hay on horses those days, you know.

And the other two,
  my dad, and another one.
    they call that—
      my dad is named Jimmy.
And the other one is named Johnny.
And Jimmy and Johnny,
  they were piling after the hay was raked, you know,
    they pile it
      so it can be ready to
        haul on the wagon, those days.
But these other two,
  one of them was raking
    and the other one was cutting hay.
The one that's cutting hay,
  his name John,
    John Kwee-LAH-kin.
That's Indian word.
And the other one,
  his name Joseph,
    Joseph Louie.
He's the one that runs the rig.
And these other two,
  my dad, his name Jimmy,
    Jimmy Robinson.
And the other one,
  Johnny Cho-WA-sket.
That's another Indian word
  in his last name.
So, one day,
  these two was working with a team.
But these other two,
  they just piling the hay
    so it can be ready to haul 'em, you know.
And then this
  one that runs the horse mower
    the time,
      about five o'clock
      in the evening.
And they were still cutting
  because those days they,
    they never quit 'til six o'clock,

233

maybe quarter to six before they quit working,
ten hours a day.
So just about five o'clock and
they not far from these two
where they cut the hay.
And those days you know,
the bar,
the cutter only four feet and a half.
And the horse mower,
they kind of light,
you know that, eh, because you seen that.
They kind of light.
And not much power in those mower[s] you know,
those days.
So these two,
they working and they
piling up the hay
and they see that teamster, they stopped.
And then they backed—
the horses, they backed—
and then go,
but still skidding.
The wheel.
And then they back it,
they could hear it when they ...
"click-click-click-click"
when they back, you know.
And then go again,
still skidding.
Well that way,
we think maybe little roots,
or maybe hard manure,
they might [be] stuck in between the guards, you know.
And then we have to get off and then look.
If it is, and it—
kick them out, or
hit 'em with a hammer, out.
And then it'll go.
So they think
maybe something like that.

They get off the machine.
And then they take hammer or something,
  to carry that,
    if it's hard—
      little roots or maybe hard manure,
        they could hammer that off.
So they can't take the ...
  pull out the grass,
    because the grass got stuck on the guards, you know.
Instead of little roots, or
  hard manure,
    there was a snake.
The big snake.
Pretty big—
  and long.
And then they wrapped there,
  they stopped the cutter.
But they never cut, never—
  no blood.
They never cut,
  they never got hurt, but they ...
    they coiled the cutter, you know
      and they stop it.

And they drive the horses, and then the
  wheel was skidding.
They never cut.
That's the one
  they stopped the cutter.
So they surprised.
They never seen that way before.
Because we—
  I, I cut the snake lots of times
    and I cut 'em in pieces, you know.
No more.

So they ...
  they call these other two,
    they want them to see
      what he seen.
So they called them,

and tell them to come.
My dad and this other man,
    they went over there and they tell them,

        "Look at that.
            That's a snake stopped this.
            That's funny."

And then they tried to
    get him out with a fork, you know,
        but no, they still there.
And Johnny, he says,

        "I'll get him out."

And then they went out little ways
    and they get the dry hay,
        bunch of dry hay,
            and then he twist it.
And they come back,
    and they take a match and light it,
        and then they put light—fire
            in the snake, you know.
And then the snake, they—
    right away, they get out.
They loosen up because it's going to burn.
Loosen up and
    away they go.
And Johnny had to get the fork,
    and they run after him—
        the big snake!
And they hit him with the fork,
    the both of them,
        they hit him with the fork,
            and they kill him.
So they ...
    they surprised, you know,
        they never see the snake stop the,
            the cutter on the mower, you see.
If they do get 'em, they cut.
They cut to pieces.

But this one, hey,
  they never got scratched.
So they quit,
  just about quitting time,
    and they go to the house.
And their boss,
  he don't work.
Kind of an old man—
  not too old, maybe
    sixty, something like that.
Anyway, they get [to] the house,
  and then they get together, and then
    they had a big table there and they ...
      sittin' there and eat.
And while they['re] eating,
  and one of these boys,
    they tell about that,
      what happened with that mower, and
        snake stop it.
They tell all about it—
  not only them, but there was some more other boys.
And they talked about it, and
  they surprised that a snake—
    they could never stop the cutter.
Or else they can be cut too.
They all talked about [it].
But the boss never said a word.
They never did say nothing.
So ...
  two weeks after that,
    and the boss was still at [the] house, you know,
      they don't work.
And one afternoon,
  afternoon, and his wife told him,

          "Maybe you should tell the boys
              and harness the team of horses
              and hook up the buggy,
            I'm going to the store
              to get some groceries."

The store was about four miles,
   from their house to the store.
All right.
They tell the boys,
   and then the boys harness the horses
     and his wife and another lady,
       they were there.
I guess they help her for the cooking, you know—
   and they went to the store.
And then the boss,
   all [by] himself in the house,
     all alone.
The others were out working.
Then his wife,
   and the extra lady,
     they go—
       the other lady—
         to the store—
           to get some groceries.
But only him
  and a little boy,
    about fourteen years old.
He run out, you know,
  they go to the blacksmith shop and they
    running around there.

But he's in the house,
  that boss,
    that Tom Daley.
The first thing he know,
  they heard a shot—
    bang!
Heard a shot.
And they put the gun right here
  and then they fire.
Through the head—
  right in the kitchen.
And then the roof is,
  it's that way,
    and then that was the kitchen,

and there was another house
   that way and then
      another house.
Seems to be the house was kind of across.
Then they right in the kitchen,
  right in the centre,
    that's where they shot themself
    and they['re] dead.
Then they heard from the
  blacksmith shop,
    not far from the house.
They heard the shot.
And then they ...
  they was wondering, you know,
   they had to go to the house
    to see what's the matter.

And then the boy, they run.
And they get to the house and open the door
  and his dad was laying right there.
And they turned around, and they
  met the blacksmith, and then they said,

     "My dad is dead!"

So the blacksmith get there,
  and they seen them—
   they died.
They shot that—
  right here,
   they come out.
So they tell the boy,

    "Take the horse
      and get on the horse
       right away and then you
        go towards the store,
          you could meet your mom on the way
          and tell her it's not good."

Not to know until she come.

"You better let her know
        before they get home."

So the boy get on the horse
    and away they go.
And they met his mom on the halfways, like
    and then they tell 'em,

        "Dad is dead.
            Shot himself."

So the lady, they knows already before she get home.
And the same boy,
    this boy was about fourteen years old.
The same boy they sent to Fairview.
That's from Tom Daley Bluff
    and then he's got to go over there ...
        you didn't know, I think, that place,
            that's where they have the rodeo nowadays
                up towards on the Fairview road.
And that road
    it leads into Oliver
        but it's just on the other side of Daley Bluff
            just from Cawston
                to the west.
They sent the same boy
    to Fairview.
That's where they['ve] got the
    policeman, and the courthouse and
        everything there.
That was [a] mining town.
So he get on the horse and then went
    to tell the policeman.
And then whoever they are, there,
    some of them white men,
        the blacksmith and some of them
            they tell 'em not to touch him.
Leave him as they are,
    right there where they was.
Just leave 'em there.
'Til the policeman come—

maybe tonight,
    maybe tomorrow.
So the boy, they get to Fairview
  late at night.
And told this
  and then the policeman said,

        "Well, we'll go
            the first thing in the morning."

And they tell the boy,

        "You not going back,
            you stay here.
        The first thing in the morning,
            early, we go."

So this boy,
  they stay there
    and also the policeman.
Next morning
  they all come.
The two policeman, and that boy.
And that night
  they kind of wait,
    some of them, they say,

        "They may not come tonight.
        Maybe in the morning."

But still, they think
  maybe they might come after a while.
And they built a fire.
That was in haying time, you know,
  like in August or September.
And they built a fire outside
  and then a lot of people there,
    lots of people stand there by the fire.
Some Indian people,
  and some white people,
    all their neighbours, they all heard that
    and then they all get together.

At night.
Like tonight, you know—
  moonlight.

And then they had a
  bunch of cat[s] in the ranch, you know,
    in the house,
      in the place.
Bunch of cat[s]
  and then one of them was a spotted cat.
I think the spotted cat is bad, anyway.
There was a spotted cat and he's
  supposed to be tom cat,
    he's a big one.
That's the bad of the cats, you know.
So the first thing you know,
  these people they had a fire away from the house
    a little ways.
The first thing you know,
  they could hear the cat,
    they was walking back and forth on the roof, you know,
      up on the ridge.
And it say,

      "Meow, meow ... "

  ... loud!

Seems to be crying.
They['re] walking
  back and forth on that ridge—
    and that's where the body—
      right down in there.
See, the roof ridge is here,
  and then they was laying right there.
In the house.
And the cat walking
  back and forth on the roof.
And the roof it's ...
  it's—you know, the house,
    and the roof it's past the building like that,
      you know.

And they could never figure out
  how that they can get up there.
But he's walking on top.
They walked there all night,
  and then they
    cry all night,

          "Meow, meow ... "

... loud!

All night.
And they stop, they quit—
  and after a while, and then again.
Pretty near morning
  they disappeared.
Nobody know where they go,
  how did they come down.
They got no idea.
They never seen them.
They not up there.
They come down.
When daylight in the morning,
  they see 'em there—
    they get down.
But nobody knew
  how did they get up and
    how they come down.
So ...
  when the policeman come,
    and they looked at him
      and tell them,

          "Well, that's all,
            he's dead.
          All you've got to do is to take him,
            and tomorrow, or next day,
              bury him."

And this man,
  he's supposed to be Catholic.
And the priest—

no church those days,
   at anywhere.
The priest,
   he comes from Penticton
      on the stage, they call 'em.
I guess you remember the stage.
The horses, you know,
   they four horses
      [and a] buggy.
Then the priest comes from Penticton on this stage
   to Keremeos.
And then they,
   they goes over there.
And they do the mass at Tom's place.
Tom's house.
Every month.
So this time,
   they thought they could call the priest
      because Tom is dead.
Anyway, they did.
The priest come.
And they had the funeral
   and they told the priest all about [it].
And they told him about this cat.
And the priest said,

      "That cat
         is trying to help him
            from going to hell."

But the cat couldn't do nothing
   because he shot himself.

He kill himself.
The cat was trying to help him
   from going to hell.
But he can't do nothing
   because they kill himself.
And then the priest said,

      "You watch that cat
         maybe two weeks,

> maybe before two weeks from now
> they'll be disappeared,
>   you can never see 'em
>   no more.
> He's going to go away.
> He's going to leave."

So they know that.
In about two weeks' time,
  no more, that spotted cat.
Nobody know which way they went,
  [if] they['re] dead, or
    go someplace, they just ...
      disappeared.
See, that's
  one way the cat done.
So that's the end of that story.

Wendy: Wow!

MAYBE THAT LAKE MIGHT BE TUNNEL

A man and his canoe go missing in Palmer Lake.
But they turn up elsewhere.

And there's another stories ...
There always be Indians,
  they camped along the Palmer Lake.
And one time they had the camp there.
And one old man, they not very old,
  he was talking about ...
    he wants to measure that lake,
      how deep it was.
And they was saying,
  they going to make a rope,
    twisted the rope, you know,
      they call that Indian rope,
        it was a grass.
And they get them
  and then they took the parts of 'em
    and they had them join 'em together
      and they twist 'em.
They twist that
  and then they connect 'em to this long stick
    and they can twist 'em.
So this old man, he get a lot of that
  and he twisted that rope.
It's not pretty—
  well, it's about this big,
    maybe smaller.
But it's long, you know.
He twist this rope and then he got lots of 'em.
So they tell 'em,

"What you going to do with that rope?"

"Well," he says,
"I'm going to measure this lake.
 I want to know how deep."

So they twist this rope
 and then they finish 'em.
Then they load 'em on the canoe.
Then they got a dog
 but maybe not as big as this one.
But got a dog, anyhow.
So they get on that canoe.
Then they put all this rope in.
Big pile in the canoe.
Then his dog.
Then they went out.
And these other people were watching 'em.
They went out
 and then they come to just about in the middle.
They look this way
 and look this way and that way
  and they went around there for a while.
I guess they figure that could be the centre.
And they got the stone
 and they tie the stone with a rope
  and then they drop them in the lake.
Then the rope keep coming
 and they going down,
  going down,
   going down.
And they watch 'em from the shore.
Then the rope, they must've get to the end.
Then they must've grab it right in the end.
And they dig down
 and they put his arm down in the water.
No more rope
 and still they never touch bottom of that lake.
So it looks like.

But nobody know.
But they thought,
  because they tip to the side.

And then, the first thing they know,
  the canoe, they just raise up.
Just like the horse when the horse would rear up, you know.
Same thing.
They just raise up.
For a little while, pretty near almost straight up
  and down it went in the water.
Dog and all and the man,
  they just disappeared.
Then they waited for a while,
  they thought maybe this canoe,
    they might float out.
They might come out on the surface of the water.
But never.
Never did seen 'em.

Just straight up and down it went,
  and no more.
But for a long time, just about next year,
  a year after that,
    and then the people were hunting up on the mountain,
      from that lake on up on the mountain.
There was some lakes up there too.
Little lakes, not pretty big.
But along the shore that little lakes,
  there's two, three up on that mountain.
And they found a piece of that canoe—
  the one that went down.
Well anyway, they not sure that was the one
  but it's a canoe.
They broke off a canoe.
They lay, and then there was a bone.
On them, you know,
  just so wide, they broke off that canoe.
So long, and then there's a bone.
Part of a bone, maybe a rib,
  or maybe this bone,

or something like that.
It's lay on that board, like.
They find 'em.
Not only in one place,
  in a few places,
    in all these little lakes up there.
So they figure that'll be the only man's canoe,
  and some of his bones.
I don't know,
  that's the way they tell.

They thought, maybe that lake,
  they might've be tunnel to another lake,
    way up on the mountain.
Maybe that's where this canoe—
Only ways they could figure.
And that's the end of that.

   Wendy: That's Palmer Lake again?

Yeah.

   Wendy: So Palmer Lake must be kind of a special lake?

It's a special lake
  and it's a bad one too.

And, maybe you stop that 'til I look for some more.

WHY NOWADAYS THE DOG CAN CHASE THE CAT

*A traveller in search of work finds himself
in a very unusual household.*

And this is a short stories.
This stories, that's way back from while they was imbellable.
But not animal.
Right after the imbellable stories.
Right after the animal people.
And this stories is not Indian.
They are white people.
And, story, gold on gold for ring.
Gold for ring.
And that's not Indian.
That's white people do that.
But it sounds like imbellable stories.
That's from way, way back.

There was a man, they travel in the prairie country
  where is just nothing but flat.
I seen those, you know, near Winnipeg.
And they great, but all level.
On that kind of place,
  somewhere, I don't know where but anyway over there,
    and they was travelling in the prairie country,
      all over.
They could see a long ways.
He don't know where he was going,
  he seems to lost.
And they was going along
  and they could see a long ways
    because it's all open
      and they all level.

And they could see long ways.
It look, kinda looks like a building, or something.
Watch 'em for a while,
  it's too far,
    they look like smoke.
But anyway, they go straight to that.
They go and they get quite a ways
  and they get near.
And by God, it looks like a building.
Looks like a house.
And they keep goin', get near,
  and they could tell it *was* a building.
So they kept a-coming.
And they get to the place.
Right in the open place,
  and there was houses there, a building.
One barn, corral, house, ranch home.
But nobody there.
When they get there.
But they looked around
  and looks like there somebody here this morning.
They're fresh track.
Maybe they just go away—
They might come back after a while,
  tonight maybe, sometime.

> "I just as well wait here.
> When they come back—
> This—it look like a ranch.
> They might give me a job."

They want to work.
So he stays.
They looked around and looks like somebody there
  but that night, there nobody there.
And they got some barn,
  and it looks like they got some horses there,
    but they go, they mighta be right out.
So he sat around 'til the night comes.
In the summer, you know, the sun is pretty high yet.

But it was about six o'clock.
Then, he could see the riders from quite a ways.
See them coming.
And he looked and watched.
And pretty soon they come.
Three man.
And they kinda surprised, this mans,
  to see a man at their place.
Because they never see nobody since they live there.
And they tell 'em,

> "Where did you come from?
>   What did you do around?"

> "Well," he says,
> "I just travel through the place
>   and the country.
>   Seems to kind of lost.
>   And I can see these building from a long ways.
>   And I thought I'd better come.
>   And I'd like to get a job,
>   if there's any job for me.
>   I could see this looks like a ranch."

So these mans, the three of them,
  they look at one another
    and they talk to one another.
Pretty soon they say,

> "Maybe all right.
>   We can get him a job.
>   Housekeeper.
>   He can look after—
>   they could stay here all the time.
>   And he can do the cooking.
>   They cook.
>   We can only eat here in the evening,
>   and in the morning.
>   But we always take our lunch for noon.
>   And he can cook twice a day.
>   Then they could sweep the floor,

wash the floor,
look after the place."

And they got some chicken.
They got some pigs.
They got some things,
they got to look after it.
But when they come back
and they feed the chicken,
they feed the pigs.
But in the morning, they do that work
and then they go.
They went out for a ride.

So he got a job.
This strange man.
Tell 'em,

"You can just stay
and you cook in the morning.
This time, in the morning,
we'll show you.
Pretty soon you get used to it
and you can do it yourself."

So they were there.
And a big house.
There was four or five room in the house.
And one room is locked.
The other room is open
and they go in and sweep the floor.
But the other room is locked.
So when the mans came home
and asked,

"Why do you guys keep that room locked?
I want to go in and sweep the floor."

So they look at one another
and they don't say.
But when they away from him, you know,
I guess they talked about it.

So finally they told him,

> "All right.
> We can open.
> We can unlock that room.
> So you can go in there.
> And do your work like the way you say,
>   sweep the floor.
> But there's one thing you could see in that house.
> Right on the ceiling,
>   just about in the middle.
> And there hanged, up there on the ceiling,
>   and it seems to look like it's dripping.
> They come down, quite a ways, and back again.
> And then they come down quite a ways.
> Supposing, they pretty near come to your head.
> And jump back again.
> They always do that.
> It's kind of a yellow."

And they tell 'em,

> "Don't touch that.
> If you touch 'em,
>   it might be bad for you.
> And you can stand and watch
>   but don't get in your body anyplace.
> Don't touch 'em.
> They might be bad for you if you do.
> But you can see."

All right.
These man go away
  and then it was unlocked.
Go in and they could see—just about in the middle—
  the yellow stuff.
Just like a—looks like a—
Supposing if you hang on the syrup, you know.
They went down
  but they wouldn't go back, you know.
They keep going down.
But this one it go down like a syrup.

254

But jump back.
After a while, he comes again.
Down so far, and then it went back.
They do that all the time.

He watch 'em for a while.
They do that all the time,
  for quite a while.
Quite a few days,
  and just stop there and stand
    and watch
      and watch.
They always do.
They come down and right back.
He was wondering,
  he got the thought,

> "One day I thought I would like to touch it with my finger.
> It looks nice.
> It look clear.
> It look nice."

But they don't know what it was.
So anyway, he thought,

> "I'll try it."

When they comes down, and—
Anyways, pretty small, you know.
So he put his finger there.
This finger.
That's why I got the ring.
Look here, that's gold.

  Harry laughs.

Look.
And he touch 'em with this finger.
That's the reason why they call that ring finger.
From that time it become to have that name.

And they touch 'em the little bit.
The first thing you know,

they were ring there.
Just in one second and there was a ring.
And they couldn't get it out.
He tried to get 'em out.
My God, he wet it and he couldn't get 'em out.
By God, they thought,

> "That's bad.
> If I get it out,
> I could hide 'em.
> They wouldn't know.
> But I can't get it out.
> They will find out—
> They going to give me heck.
> They might fire me."

Anyway, they get some rag.
And they rub it up with a rag,
  right over here.
They rub 'em up.
And they get some juice,
  like some strawberry juice
    or some kind of a red juice,
      and they paint it, you know.
So they could look like a blood.
So they tie 'em that way
  and then when the boys come back
    and they seen 'em,
      the finger wrapped up.

> "What's the matter with you?"

He's got a name,
  but I forget his name.

> "Oh," he says.
> "I was cooking
>   and I was cuttin' the meat
>   and then I had 'em cut.
>   I got the cut
>   and that's why."

So they kind of believed him,
  the first time, you know.
But later on, that they find out,
  they touch that.
There was a ring.
They cover that.
And they going to get 'em.
And take that off from him.
Or they going to kill him or something.

So they run away.
Try to get away.
And they chased him.
Just whole three of 'em,
  chased him and pretty soon,
    the other two that's in behind,
      they give up.

But the one is on the lead,
  they keep chasing him.
They run and run and run for long ways.
And then they come to a place
  where they can see another building.
And, there was building
  and there was some rags and canvas and stuff,
    it was kind of piled on the outside of the barn or house.
And they get there.
And they, whoever they chased 'em,
  is quite a ways behind 'em.
But, they getting played out.
Pretty tired.
So they changed himself into a mouse.
Then they get under that bunch of canvas,
  it was laying.
They get under there.
Changed himself into a mouse.
And this one come.
And they went around.
And they know they get under there.
They know they changed to be a mouse.

All right.
This one here they thought,
  they can change to be a cat.
And they changed to be a cat,
  and they know where they get under—this mouse.
And they stand back and set there and watch.
If it comes out, they going to grab 'em.
They watch there.
They don't look anywhere but only there.
They keep his eyes steady there.
But the mouse, they go the other way.
And they come out of the—
  underneath, in the different place.
And they peek out and look,
  and this one,
    they watching there all the time.
And they turned back and they get up
  and they changed himself into a dog.

And then they, the cat was looking that way,
  'til they come behind and jumped on 'em
    and grab 'em.
Grab the cat.
Kill 'em.

So they kill 'em all right.
That was the one that they got the ring.
He is the one,
  they turn into a dog.
And kill the cat.
But, it says, the sound that they hear,
  it says,

        "Well, that was all right for now.
         You kill 'em.
         But not all the time.
         Should not be that way all the time.
         Just only now.
         But later on, maybe once in a while,
         It can happen that way."

But the dog can always chase the cat.
But they could never caught up to 'em.
The cat can always got away.
Or else, if they caught up to 'em,
  if they got no place to climb,
    and caught up to 'em,
      and the cat can roll down
        and they gonna grab it
          and the cats could scratch 'em on the mouth
          with his sharp needles.
Then the dog wouldn't kill 'em.
In the otherwise,
  that way the dog would scared, you know,
    they might—
      his nose bleeding by scratch.
And they stop.
And the cat'll stop
  and then pretty soon
    they'll be friends.
They don't have to kill one another.

But once in a while,
  they might kill one cat.
Not all the time.
That is why nowadays,
  look at last night,
    your dog did this to my cat.
And they do that.
Any dog.
Like a strange cat.
They always chase 'em.
But if the people here,
  if I had a cat here,
    then I could get a dog,
      a little pup maybe,
        and pretty soon they acquaint one another,
        and they friends.
They wouldn't fight.
They all right.

He know, he can step over.

He likes to lay down where it's cooler,
  over there.

So that's the way it happens.
That's why nowadays the dog can chase cat.
But they never caught up to 'em.
Chase 'em 'til the cat got away.
Or sometimes the cat with no chance to climb to a tree,
  and the dog caught up to 'em,
    and they just lay down.
And the dog want to grab 'em,
  but they scratch 'em.
They once or twice scratch 'em,
  and they bleeding,
    then the dog got away.
Then he get up
  and then they hump his back
    and they show the dog he is better than him, you know.
So they don't kill one another.
So, that's all.

THEY FIND THAT MAN BY HIS POWER

An Indian doctor finds a missing man.

Now, here's the stories,
  it's just the short stories.
There was a man,
  a man who was found—
    well, a man who was missing.
Supposed to be hunting.
They went up on the logging road.
From Nespelem up on the mountain.
They went up on the logging road.
Supposed to be hunting, but they were missing.
They never come back for three, four days.
And they look for him.
And they look for it and they find the camp.
They find his camp.
But they never find him.
They look for it,
  and a bunch of people,
    they look for it all over
      and then they couldn't find it.
And they was celebrating, that time.
I was there.
I was in Nespelem and I heard about that.

So, they couldn't find him,
  and then they thought,
    they going to get the dogs.
The police dogs.
See if they can find the tracks.
They might go someplace
  and maybe they got shot
    or maybe shot themselves

or maybe somebody kill 'em.
They get the dogs.
And the dog running 'round.
And they went along and they come to a lake.
Little—
  but not little,
    but the lake is not too big.
And the dog, they go around the lake about halfways.
Then they stop.
Then they sittin' there
  and then they look at the lake.
And their master tell 'em to keep going.
But they wouldn't go anymore.
They get back from there.
And they come back
  and then they talked about it
    and then they sent them out again.
The dogs, the two of them.

Then they go.
Just about halfways in the lake,
  like at the shore,
    and then they stop
      and they be sitting there
        and they look to the left.
And then come back.
So, they thought,
  well, the dogs, they couldn't find 'em.
They couldn't do much.
Might as well get the bear.
Somebody got the bear, you know.
At home.
Two of them bears.
Somebody tell 'em,
  the bear, they good,
    maybe better than dogs.
Take them.
See, this bear, they only yearling.
The both of 'em.
Twin bears.
So they get these bear.

And took 'em up there.
And then showed 'em the camp.
Then they showed them, you know,
  they could look around for which way they went
    when they left the camp.
And the bear, they keep going around
  and pretty soon they go to the lake.
That the same way as the dog.
They go on the lake
  and then they went along the shore about halfways,
    then they stop.
Stop,
  and then they facing to the left,
    then they look that way.
Then they started to play.
They play together.
And then they bring back
  and one of these man, they said,

       "Send 'em on this side.
        Maybe they can do something.
        Maybe better that way."

So they sent 'em on the other side of the lake.
And it went just about halfways
  and then they stop.
And then they look [at] one another
  and then they play
    and then they look to the lake.
They couldn't go anymore.
Still they couldn't do nothing.
Finally they say,

       "Maybe we should go get the Indian doctor from Montana."

There was one Indian doctor there,
  is supposed to be good Indian doctor.
He lives in Elmo, Montana.
That's quite a ways,
  that's about good ten hours drive from Nespelem to Elmo.
I've been there.
Long ways.

So, anyway, they sent the man
  and they went to get the Indian doctor.
The car went there.
They bring the Indian doctor.
We still there in Nespelem.
We were celebrating, stick game and so on.
Four, five days—you know that.
And then this happen.
We know that.
We heard about it.
So, they bring that Indian doctor.
And they take him up to that lake.
And they told him all about the dogs
  and the bear
    and they take him to that missing man's camp.
So they walked around and they sing his song.
And then they go 'round,
  go around the lake.
They go right around.
They didn't do like the dog or the bear, you know.
They go right around the lake.
And then, they come back
  and they go the camp.
Sing his song.
He said,

> "I can't see anything,
>   but maybe I leave it as it is 'til night come.
>   I go to bed.
>   I go to sleep here.
>   Maybe in the morning, might be different.
>   I might see something at night."

So they, the Indian doctor, they stay there
  and some others with 'em
  and then they sleep.
That night, towards morning,
  they started to sing his song.
He sing his song 'til the sun comes up.
From, likely from two o'clock in the morning,
  and then they sing the song,

they sing the song,
   they never stop sing the song.
'Til the sun comes up.
But up on the mountain high,
  because the sun, it'll come up early.
Anyway, they keep singing 'til the sun comes up.

After that, he says,

      "That man is in that lake,
        in the bottom of that lake.
        All you've got to do is get a hook of some kind,
         the lake is not pretty deep.
      You can go out in the boat
        and then you could scratch around.
      You might get 'em.
      You might caught 'em on your—
        the hook or—
      He's there."

So they take the boat.
They went to get the canoe, you know.
Bunch of man, maybe three, four canoe.
They got the hooks.
They make a hook but they put 'em on the rope, you know,
  so they could drag 'em around.
Finally they got 'em hooked.
Something.
Then they raise it.
And they come up to the surface of the water.
It's heavy.
And this man was been tied on with a big stone,
  kind of lead stone,
    and a big one.
And they was tied on there with a wire.
Whoever, they tie 'em on
  and tie 'em pretty good
    on the stone with a wire
      and then they must've—
They must have a canoe
  and then they might've go out in the middle of the lake.

Right in the centre,
  and then they dropped him.
Nobody can find him.
But only the Indian doctor.

They find that by his power, you know.
They sleep that night.
And then towards morning they sing 'til the sun goes up.
And then they find out where that man was.
And then they went over there
  and then they find 'em from that.
So that's the end of that story.

WHEN I FIRST REMEMBER ...

Harry has a vivid first memory.

What I was going to say ...
I was going to say about this,
  the very few words of, in my first beginning,
    when I first remember.
I, Harry Robinson, I'm eighty-four years old.
Now, this year, in 1984.
But I remember at the time, was in 1903.
And that something important to me.
  I asked quite a few people like my age, or else older, or else younger.
See if they remembers when they were three years old
  and up to grown up.
But, I never find any.
They remembers when it's four or five.
Usually, five years old before they could to remember.
But I remember when I was three years old.
It was in 1903.

We had a camp in one place in fall time,
  like in October.
Must be—I can't see how do I know it was October at that time.
But I can see the leaves were falling off from the trees.
From the cottonwood tree, from the poplar tree.
So that must've been October month, at that time.
And we had a camp,
  and I and mother, and her mother—
    her mother was old and blind.
And we just the four.
We just the three of them.
My grandfather—but at this time was away for a few days.
And, one morning my mother, she says,
  I heard 'em go to her mother,
    and they have to go close to her mother's ears

to talk to 'em, because the old lady is deaf and blind.
Can't see and they can't hear.
They went close to her mother's ears
  and tell her, they going to leave us for that day.
She's going, about mile or mile and a half for our neighbour.
To give 'em a hand working digging potatoes or vegetables,
  things like that at that day.
But she'll be back in the evening time
  and not too late.
Maybe about five o'clock, something like that.
They'll be back.
That's what she says to her mother.
I heard 'em saying that.

And she left.
She go walk.
They leave and I see 'em walking.
And that day, I been playing around and she tell me,

> "Don't you go too far away from old lady.
>   They might want you.
>   They might call you, then you could give 'em something.
>   Maybe want the water or something like that.
>   Don't go too far away."

All right.
I play right around close.
And then, on that day she is supposed to come back
  'til the sun shine.
It could be halfways up to the hillside to the east.
That means about five o'clock.
But they come back early.
I seen 'em coming.
On horseback.
But they left—
She go walking, when they left.
But she come back on horseback.
And I can tell that was my mother.
And when she get to the camp and get off the horse
  and tie the horse, I ask her.
I says,

"How come were you there on that horse?"

She says to me,

> "Never mind.
> I'm going to tell the old lady about that.
> And just sit there and listen."

All right.
She went then and talked to her mother.
That was my grandmother.
And I listened to her.
She says to her mother,

> "I come back to get you and your grandson."

That was me.

> "I bring the horse.
> A gentle horse.
> And I'm going to put you on that horse
>   and your grandson, put 'em on behind you on the saddle.
> Then I could to lead you.
> From here to our neighbour."

Because my grandmother ...

Tape cuts out here for a few seconds.

Shkway-at-KANE, that's the man's name.
They got killed that day.
And he died and they gonna bring him at his home.
And there's a lot of people goes over there.
There'll be a funeral maybe next couple of days.
But they goin' over there that night.
Left us at our neighbour, to Mrs. Qualtier.

Mrs. Qualtier, they got too many little kids.
They can't be away.
And they got one comin', you know, they gettin' kinda big.
And then they just got to stay home.
So that's where we'll be.

My mother tell her mother that and I listen.

I know what she says all about.
And my mother [means grandmother]says,

   "Maybe that horse, I might fall off."

And my mother says,

   "No, they really old horse and really gentle.
   You can ride. I can put you on.
   I can help you to get on and your grandson behind you.
   And I tie you together with the rope so nobody can fall.
   Then I can lead you.
   When we get to our neighbour, then you get off
     and you best have to stay for about three or four days
       with Mrs. Qualtier.
   But I and William Qualtier, we ride and we go over there.
   And maybe tomorrow sometimes, maybe William come back.
   Or maybe I come to see what's going on and then I go again."

I heard 'em saying that.

So they did.

They put her on the horse.
And they put me behind my grandma and then they tie us together
  with a light blanket.
And they lead the horse and we on the horse, I and my grandmother.
When we come to our neighbour's place
  and we getting off,
    and Mrs. Qualtier they were glad that we get
      there because the grandmother could talk to her,
        tell her some stories and one thing and another.
She like that.
So there were some kids there for me to play with.
So that was good.
So we stay there.

And I remember that at that time in the fall time in about October in 1903.

When I become to be a man,
  when I was about seventeen years old, myself,
    then I said to my mother,

      "I remember that."

And I says to my mother,

> "This is what you do that time.
> You go over there to work for the day but you didn't work
>   all day.
> You come back with that horse and me behind her.
> And you tie us together with a light blanket.
> And you leave us at Mrs. Qualtier.
> And then you and William go to funeral to where the people
>   gather,
> > not too far, about six, seven miles from there
> > where Shkway-at-KANE got killed.
> > I remember that."

My mother looked at me.
Gave me a good lookin' for a while.
Then she said,

> "Did you remember that?"

I says,

> "I do."

She says,

> "You are right. You tell the right stories."

So that was my proof that I remember when I was three years old.

See? I was born on October 8, 1900.
So that shows that I did remember when I was three years old.
But I asked so many girls and boys, old men and a lot of people
  if they remember like I do on the certain number of years.
But they don't.
They remember when they five years old.
And they might remember just here and there when they's four.
But when I was three, I remember all that.
Not all through but just there.
But after that I don't remember.
Just part. Just in certain places.

So that will be all for now.

STEALING HORSES FROM THE BLACKFOOT

Some Okanagan Indians play a crafty trick on the Blackfoot when the latter deny them horses.

Long time ago, no horses here.
They didn't see horses.
Never seen 'em.
But, this is not the Indian stories,
  this is, the white man told me that.
They say, Mexico, and Spain.
That was Spain that was the first—
The Spain—they comes across the lake from Spain
  and they landed where the Mexico is now.
But it was the Spain at that time
  when they first landed there.
Before the white people.
Before the French.
And that was the first.
They was going to land it way, this way.
But, from Spain and they went on the lake,
  on the boat,
    and they move by wind, you know.
Because only light boat those days.
Not too big, you know.
And the wind was blowing,
  and the wave,
    and the first thing they know,
      they were a way down.
Before they landed.
Way down where is Mexico is now.

And, for a while,
  and they got the bigger boat,
    and they always come across

and go back.
And they got a lot of horses over there.
So they thought they going to bring some horses
  in where the Mexico is.
And when they landed,
  at the Mexico,
    and there was a lot of Indians.
Right there.
A lot of Indians.
And the Spain, get there.
And then they mix to the Indians.
And they still mix.
And that's why they call 'em Mexico.
Because they *mix* with the Indian.
Then, even today, they seems to be all Mexico
  but they, in the first place,
    it was part Indian.
Half-Indian and half-Spain.
But he turn into half-and-half.
And that's why they got the name of Mexico.
So that's what the white man told me.

Then, they bring the horses.
Course, that Spain is not cold country.
It's kind of warm anyway.
And when they get the horses to where Mexico is now,
  and that's still too warm—
    too far down.
Then they use the horses,
  but they turn loose the others, you know.
They let them run in range.
And the horses increase.
And pretty soon they got a lot of horses.
They nobody's horses.
They no brand or nothing.
They just a bunch of horses,
  just increase itself.
And that place is too warm.
For the horses.
Then the horses, they could smell the north wind.
Blow—the wind was blowing from the north.

And they could smell the north wind.
Then they go that way,
  towards the wind.
It's cooler.
So they like to go where it's cooler.
That's too warm for them.
So they kept a-coming.
And they kept a-coming,
  up, up, up,
    in the mountain, like.
Along from Mexico and Colorado and all that.
Not this way,
  but just in the meadowland.
Where it's high.
And they kept a-coming
  'til they get to the Blackfoot.
Where the Browning is now.
And there was a lot of Indians there.
The Blackfoot Indian.
Even today there's a lot of Indians over there.

And, they seen these horses.
Then the white people,
  they come from the east
    and they keep moving, you know.
Moving to the west.
And a lot of 'em come by there.
They come by this bunch of Indians—
  that Blackfoot.
And the white people told the Indians,

        "There's a lot of horses there—
          you should get some
          and break 'em
            and you could use 'em.
        You can ride 'em.
        You can pack 'em.
        You can use it for anything."

So finally the white people,
  they help the Indian

and they get the horses.
They chase 'em around
  and they rope them,
    and then they got 'em
      and then they broke 'em,
        and then they halter broke 'em
          and pretty soon the Indians,
            they get used to get horses.

And that's how come the Indians over there,
  in the Blackfoot,
    this is the first Indians to get some horses.
But not here yet.
And these Indians,
  these Okanagan right from Nespelem,
    and Spokane Indian, all that.
They heard about these horses.
The Blackfoot, they got some horses.
So they thought maybe they should go over there
  and buy some horses.
But no money, you know, those days.
But they got some—
They made some moccasins
  and made the blanket, like, out of the skin.
And they use—
They got the teepee, all hide,
  buckskin hide, you know, and all that.
They packs that and they move to,
  to the Blackfoot.
They want to trade that for horses.
They give 'em that stuff.
They make the clothes out of the buckskin, you know.
Shirt or pants, moccasins,
  things like that.
Pack them there.
They give 'em to Blackfoot Indian, but they figure they
  going to give 'em horses.
But the Blackfoot wouldn't give the horses away.
They don't want to sell 'em.
They say to the Okanagan,

"We're not stuck for clothes.
  We kill the buffalo.
    And we use the buffalo skin
     and we kill the antelope,
      and then we use that skin for clothes.
  And we not stuck.
  We don't care.
  We're not going to let you have the horses."

So that sounds not good, you know,
  to the Okanagan.
And finally the Okanagan,
  they thought,

    · "Well, they wouldn't sell us the horses, ·
     they wouldn't give the horses to us,
      but we can go over there and get 'em.
    We're going to stole it from them.
    If they're good enough,
     they kill us.
    If they're not, we kill 'em."

So that means, it's going to be war.
So the Indians from Nespelem and also from Spokane,
  they call that *Spo-ken-eh*,
    that's why the white people call 'em Spokane nowadays.
And a lot of these power mans,
  a bunch of 'em, and in winter time,
    about this time of year,
     maybe like in January,
      when it's the middle of winter.
Then they sing their song.
Sing their song
  and they beat the drums,
    just like I did last night.
And then they—
When they beat the drum, in one teepee,
  and then there's a lot of teepee, you know.
And they heard, maybe someone,
  maybe only one man,
    and they beat the drum
     and they sing the song.

War song.
Then, one of them,
  they go over there,
    they thought they better go over there
      and join that man.
Then they come in,
  then they got the drum,
    and then they beat the drum.
And the other one,
  they go over there
    and they join this.
Pretty soon they getting to be big bunch.
All mans.
And womans too.
Then, towards spring and they big bunch, you know.
So that means, in the summer,
  they can move.
To the Blackfoot.
And they can try to get horses.
Or else they can fight.
One way or the other.
Or everything will be killed over there,
  or bring the horses.
One or the other.

So they, in springtime, in summer, when it gets—
  because it's got to go over so many mountains, you know.
When that snow no more.
Then they move.
From Nespelem and they walked all the way
  to Browning is now.
That's a long way, for walking.
Then they gets to—
There's a lot of Blackfoot, maybe one camp,
  and another camp in certain places, you know.
Then they get there
  and then they hide,
    they sneak.
Then they could see this is camp.
Then they watch the camp from the distance
  because it's all open.

Over there in the prairie,
  I guess you seen 'em,
    the little bushes, about this high—
      that's all.
That not like this, over there.
But they go in and hide.
Then they figure out,
  how they going to get the horses.
And there's only two, three man that
  they can get the horses.
Not the others.

One of 'em is named Klee-OUT-kin.
That's his Indian name.
Klee-OUT-kin.
He's Okanagan Indian.
Half-Okanagan Indian and half-Blackfoot.
So that's the kind of man he was.
And he was a power man too.
And one time they were there for long time
  and he get hungry.
Nothing to eat, you know,
  they run out of food
    and some 'em they come back
      and then they give up
        and they couldn't get horses.
And they come back.
They can hunt on the way coming
  so they can eat something.
But these others,
  is only about three, four man.
Stay there.
They still taking a chance to get some horses.
Five or six man.
And they all power man,
  Indian doctors, what it's left there.
And they tell one another,

        "You'll have to do your best
          so we can get horses."

And, he says,

>"I don't think I can do it,
>>anything better."

Then they asks the other one,

>"Maybe you should try your best."

They keep saying that to one another.
Finally they tell that Klee-OUT-kin,

>"What about you?
>You should do your best,
>>so we get some horses."

They said,

>"All right.
>If you guys take my word
>and I'll do it."

>"Well," they said,
>"You better do it.
>Otherwise we going to be starving—
>>nothing to eat."

Said,

>"I can go
>and I can get some food."

>"All right.
>You better go."

That night, you know.
And the teepee, that's why the teepee nowadays,
  well, maybe they don't do that nowadays,
    but long time ago,
      they got the teepee right in the circle.
And they big one, big circle.
They big circle,
  then they big field in the centre, like.

And that's where they have the horses.
The good horses.
Good running horses.
These horses they ride to chase the buffalo.
They can run fast.
They go like racehorses.
And they had that.
And they tie 'em up with a rope.
Then they stick the stick inside the teepee.
But the teepee, they raise, you know,
  so the rope can come right out.
But the stick is inside.
And that's why the rope was tied.
And the horses was tied on the front leg or halter.
Then they feed outside.
But the good horses,
  all the good horses in the teepee.
So nobody can get 'em.

But Klee-OUT-kin, they get that.
So, the first they do,
  they were hungry
    and the first they do,
      they said to their friends,

        "I'm going over there to see if I can find some food.
        We going to have something to eat."

Getting dark, you know.
In the summer time.
So they went.
They watch 'em.
They could see 'em going.
Not too far, and disappearing.
They couldn't see 'em no more.
But still it's open.
Still daylight, but getting pretty dark,
  is not dark yet.
They could still see 'em going,
    but not too far and they just disappear—
      they don't see 'em no more.
Then he walks 'til he come to the teepee.

Then he walking
  then he meet somebody go by,
    go that way so they wouldn't hit 'em.
You know, they never seen 'em.
Then they come to one teepee.
And then they looked all around
  and they watch where they can get the food.
And they come to one teepee.
Looked and there's a bunch of man in there.
Lay down, they all lay down in the back, you know.
They all lay down.
And the woman, is only one woman,
  they were cooking.
They got a big pot,
  a copper pot, you know.
Great big one.
I seen them, a long time ago.
Them pot more like a washing keg, you know.
About this size.
Copper.
That's where they cook the buffalo.
They cop them with the axe
  and they cut 'em, you know,
    and they cook 'em in one big pot.
And they cut 'em in big, big chunks.
And they cook them.

Then, Klee-OUT-kin, they get near.
Then the doorway, it's open
  because it's warm in the summer.
And they get in there
  and he sat right by the door.
Right where they goes in
  and he sat right there.
And this bunch of man, they all lay there—
They never seen 'em.
Because they was by the fire.
And this woman is facing that way.
And he picks up the cooking, you know.
They got the long stick,
  sharp stick,

and they take 'em out
  and look and see if it's cooked.
And they watch 'em there
  and then they got a blanket.
But nobody seen 'em.
And finally the old lady get up
  and then they get a kind of a canvas, you know,
    or something,
      and they put it along there
        and then they drag this pot, you know,   ·
          where the meat was cooked,
            and they set it there
              and then they get that sharp stick,
                and then they get one chunk
                  and put 'em over here,
                    to her side, like this way,
                      towards the back.
Then they get another one
  and they put 'em this way.
Then, when they lay them there
  and pretty soon all the water,
    they run, you know,
      and then they kind of dry
        and then cool off.
Then this mans should get up and eat that.
And finally they put them over here in a pile.
But they never looked over there.
They just get some of 'em—
  and just put 'em without seeing 'em
    and then they get another one.

And then Klee-OUT-kin, from over there,
  they slide little bit
    and then they picks up his blanket
      and they make kind of a pocket,
        right here.
As soon as that lady puts that chunk of meat down,
  then they picked 'em up
    and then they put 'em on
      and then the other one,
        they put them there.

They keep doing that
  and that they could watch.
Pretty soon they empty
  and then they could take that stick
    and then they feel around with the stick,
      see if there any more.

Well, Klee-OUT-kin, he thinks,
  there no more meat
    and he got a big bunch on his—
And he get up.
And he hold that.
And he get up and went out.
And stand there.
They watched to see what this lady got to say
  when they look back.
So they stood there awhile
  and this lady, they slide that pot to the fire.
Turn around and look at the meat
  that they piled there.
And it's not there.
But the rag was wet.
Because they come from the water
  and then put them over there
    and the rag was wet.
But no meat.
Where'd the meat go?
Not there.

Because Klee-OUT-kin, they pick 'em up
  and had 'em in his blanket.
Outside, they wait there awhile.
Then, he surprise.
Where is the meat?
And they told these mans, says,

          "You guys better get up and—
            I put a lot of meat over there
              and it's not there."

They all get up and look.
There still be lots of water.

They still wet, the rag was.
But no meat.
And one of 'em, he says,

      "Maybe dog.
        Maybe the dog ate 'em."

Oh no.
The other one says,

      "They could be—
        The dog couldn't get it.
        Because it's hot.
        They's boiling.
        They're hot when they put them there.
        The dog, they could never grab the hot.
        If they do, if it's not hot,
          they can take only one piece
            and go away.
        Maybe two, three dogs,
          they can all have one piece,
            but still they should be there, left.
        Must've be somebody.
        Must've be person, took that."

And Klee-OUT-kin was stood there,
  listen.
But they never seen 'em.
So they know what's all about
  and then he walked.
Then they had 'em outside 'em
  and running 'round
    and then they tell the other ones
      and then they tell one another what happened
      and they look around,
        see if they can see any strange,
          but nothing.
So Klee-OUT-kin went back to his friend
  and he get there and he get big bunch of meat.
All cooked.
Then they put them down
  and they eat and eat.

Then they see the horses.
While they were there,
  and they see the horses
    was tied up inside the teepee.
But the teepee was raised.
And he size the horses.
Sized up—this is a good horse here,
  and this one—all that.
They know where.
After they eat,
  and they finish that,
    then they fill up,
      and that is do 'em for a few days,
        he tell their friends,

          "We get the horses after a while
            when they sleeping.
          Then we go over there
            and we get horses."

They supposed to be—
  they supposed to be four of them.
And each one can get three horses.
They ride on one,
  and lead the two.
And the other one the same.
And the other one the same.
Four man, how many horses they do?
Three horses to each man,
  and for four man?

    Wendy: How many horses per man?

Twelve.
Yeah, twelve horses.
And, nighttime, about middle night
  or little more,
    maybe towards morning,
      and they all get there.
Then Klee-OUT-kin—
They all had a knife.
And they cut the rope.

And this rope was rawhide rope,
  they make that out of the rawhide.
Good rope.
Cut them with a knife.
And he says to another one,

> "You ride this horse
>   and then you lead these two.
> And you ride on this horse
>   and you lead the two.
> And, all of you.
> Then you can go slow.
> Not to go fast, this time.
> Just take it easy.
> And I'll be still here.
> 'Til you fellas go little ways—
>   two, three hundred yards.
> And then I can ride.
> And I can holler.
> Wake 'em up.
> Then we all run."

All right.
This other bunch, the other bunch, you know,
  they took the horses
    and go slow—
They don't go fast,
  they go easy.
'Til they get out about two, three hundred yards.
And they're out—
They wait awhile.
And here on a horse,
  they got two, three leading.
Then they think their friend is quite a ways already.
Then they holler.
They holler loud.
Then they said,

> "Klee-OUT-kin, he was here
>   and take your horses."

And away he goes!

They could hear the horses running.
Then before they get up to these others
  and they holler up.
And the Blackfoot, they get excited
  and look for horses,
    and the best horses they got,
      they were gone.
But they get the other horses,
  that not so good.
But they ride those and run up.
They run up to—
  if they catch 'em and kill 'em.
But they couldn't caught up to 'em.
Because they got the best horses.
But the Blackfoot, the horses they riding,
  they not so good as these horse was stole.
So they beat the Blackfoot.
And they bring the horses.
Not only that time,
  but there's a lot of times,
    do that.

Quite a few times they bring the horses ...
Okanagans got more power than the Blackfoot.
So that's how come they have horses in the Okanagan.
Because Klee-OUT-kin,
  they stole the horses from Blackfoot.

Then, when they get them here,
  then they had 'em increase.
Then, pretty soon they got too many horses.
Then they have to kill 'em.
And eat 'em.
Yeah, they butcher 'em.
And they eat 'em.
They good meat.
I eat horse meat.

   Wendy: What does it taste like?

It taste pretty good.
It seems to me kind of sweet.

Kind of tastes kind of a sweet.
And pretty tender.
It's kind of soft.
They pretty good eating.
They was roasting—
  they roasting 'em, you know,
    on the stick.
In open fire.
Then, another woman,
  they roasting 'em in the oven, you know,
    in the stove.
Then, us cowboy, we riding
  and we get back
    and they give us something to eat—
By God, that meat, it look nice.
We don't know what it was
  and we eating
    and they kind of smile,
      and her and old man, you know,
        said,

      "What you think of that meat?"

      "Oh, they good."

      "Do you know what that is?"

      "Well, it's deer meat."

      "Yeah," they says,

So that's the way the horses gets here.